Mastering
Academic Language

Mastering Academic Language

**A Framework for Supporting
Student Achievement**

Debbie Zacarian

CORWIN

A SAGE Company

CORWIN
A SAGE Company

FOR INFORMATION:

Corwin

A SAGE Company

2455 Teller Road

Thousand Oaks, California 91320

(800) 233-9936

www.corwin.com

SAGE Publications Ltd.

1 Oliver's Yard

55 City Road

London EC1Y 1SP

United Kingdom

SAGE Publications India Pvt. Ltd.

B 1/I 1 Mohan Cooperative Industrial Area

Mathura Road, New Delhi 110 044

India

SAGE Publications Asia-Pacific Pte. Ltd.

3 Church Street

#10-04 Samsung Hub

Singapore 049483

Printed in the United States of America

A catalog record of this book is available from the Library of Congress.

ISBN 978-1-4522-5543-9

Acquisitions Editor: Dan Alpert

Associate Editor: Megan Bedell

Editorial Assistant: Heidi Arndt

Production Editor: Cassandra Margaret Seibel

Copy Editor: Sarah J. Duffy

Typesetter: C&M Digitals (P) Ltd.

Proofreader: Caryne Brown

Indexer: Virgil Diodato

Cover Designer: Karine Hovsepian

Permissions Editor: Karen Ehrmann

This book is printed on acid-free paper.

SUSTAINABLE FORESTRY INITIATIVE
Certified Chain of Custody
Promoting Sustainable Forestry
www.sfiprogram.org
SFI-01268
SFI label applies to text stock

12 13 14 15 16 10 9 8 7 6 5 4 3 2 1

Table of Contents

Acknowledgments

To Dan Alpert, trusted editor, who made this book possible

To Francis Bailey, Judie Haynes, Audrey Morse, Ken Pransky, Barbara Passo, and Barbara Rothenberg, friends and colleagues, who graciously read my work and provide invaluable advice

To the reviewers, who took time away from their busy lives to strengthen the manuscript

To Cassandra Seibel, Sarah Duffy, and Heidi Arndt at Corwin/Sage, who made my words shine

And to my husband, Matt, for his steadfast trust, love, patience, and understanding

PUBLISHER'S ACKNOWLEDGMENTS

Corwin gratefully acknowledges the contributions of the following reviewers:

Aida Alanis
Assistant Director, Department of ELLs
Austin Independent School District
Austin, TX

Kristina Anstrom
Assistant Director
The George Washington University Center for Equity and Excellence in Education
Arlington, VA

Maria Campanario-Araica
Senior Program Director, ELL
Boston Public Schools
Boston, MA

Bruce Clemmer
Director 1, ELLP
Clark County School District
Las Vegas, NV

Michael Clyne
Teacher
Kanoheda Elementary School
Lawrenceville, GA

Michelle Da Costa
Bilingual Resource Teacher
Framingham Public Schools
Framingham, MA

Maria H. Gillentine
Title III Program Specialist
Gwinnett County Public Schools
Suwanee, GA

Christine Landwehrle
Assistant Director, Curriculum and Professional Development
SAU # 39
Amherst, NH

Katherine Lobo
ESL Teacher and Teacher Trainer
Belmont Public Schools
Belmont, MA

Jen Paul
ELL Assessment Consultant
Michigan Department of Education
Lansing, MI

About the Author

 **Debbie Zacarian,** EdD, has authored numerous publications, including *The Essential Guide for Educating Beginning English Learners* (2012), *Transforming Schools for English Learners: A Comprehensive Framework for School Leaders* (2011), and *Teaching English Language Learners Across the Content Areas* (2010), and she was a columnist for TESOL's *Essential Teacher.* A national expert in policies and practices, she cowrote the Massachusetts Department of Early Education and Care's policies for dual language learners; wrote *Serving English Learners: Laws, Policies, and Regulations,* a user-friendly guide about U.S. federal laws, a project funded with support from the Carnegie Foundation for Colorín Colorado; and served as an expert consultant with the Kindergarten Entry Assessment Advisory Committee of the Delaware Governor's Office, Delaware Children's Department, and Delaware's Office of Education. With over three decades of combined experience directing a professional development and consulting center at an educational service agency about working with culturally and linguistically diverse populations, administering public school English learner programs, serving on the faculty of the University of Massachusetts Amherst, and engaging in various state and national initiatives, Dr. Zacarian consults with state agencies and school districts in the United States on policies, programming, and professional development for culturally and linguistically diverse populations.

Introduction

Academic achievement is often characterized by measuring overall student performance on high-stakes testing as well as the percentage of students graduating high school. These numbers have provided us with a wealth of information, and much of it does not paint a promising picture. Whether we measure achievement by test scores or graduation rates, the numbers have not changed significantly—even though we have employed various interventions, including reading, writing, and math programs that are "guaranteed" to improve performance. Nor has the charter school movement done much to change the picture. Much has been written about improving academic achievement among socioeconomically, racially, culturally, and linguistically diverse populations. Some of that writing, including by this author, have focused on culturally responsive practices and English learners. In addition, other resources have focused on reflective practices when teaching racially and economically diverse populations.

This book provides a much-needed source for understanding the achievement gap as an academic language gap among what are commonly referred to as standard versus nonstandard speakers of school language and for providing ways to address it at the point of planning and delivery to create high-quality learning, school, and parent engagement environments. Mastering academic language is key for school success and, most important, for closing the achievement gap. This book provides a way of looking at achievement using an asset-based model of students who possess school-matched language skills and carry this academic language to, in, and from school, and students who are learning academic language while simultaneously attending school. It draws from the four-pronged framework presented by Collier (1995), and expanded by me (Zacarian, 2011), to describe what constitutes a high-quality learning environment in which learners of academic language can become users of academic language and flourish in school settings. The four-pronged framework describes how academic language learning is a (1) sociocultural, (2) developmental,

(3) academic, and (4) cognitive thinking-to-learn process. The prongs, as seen in the figure below, are akin to a large four-pronged electrical outlet. Each prong is essential for the electricity to turn on. Together, the four prongs discussed here are intended to be a comprehensive framework for advancing student achievement. The book describes what can be done to strategically plan and deliver high-quality learning, school, and parent engagement environments using this four-pronged framework for addressing the persistent challenge of closing the achievement gap.

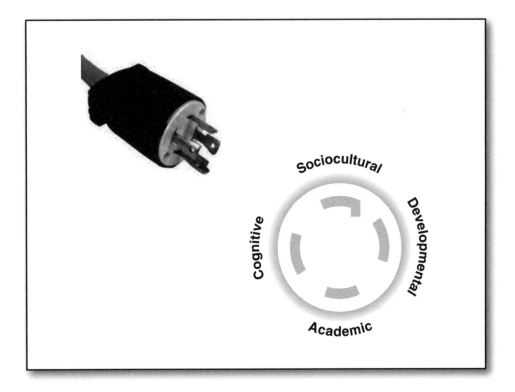

An important concept of the book is that it is intended for individual study as well as creating a collaborative conversation among teams (such as professional study groups, college classrooms that use team or small group work, book groups, and other groups) to engage in what I refer to as an *our-o-logue*. An our-o-logue is a type of interaction in which all participants are valued as rich resources and make important contributions to this vital work, as opposed to a my-o-logue, in which one person is the all-knowing authority, or a di-o-logue, in which two people actively interact back and forth while the rest of the group listens passively. Our-o-logue participants include pre- and inservice teachers, school leaders, specialists, and outreach workers, as well as parents, students, and community members who gather together for the purpose of sharing ideas, resources, and other important ways of thinking to help support the advancement of student achievement. The credo "many fingers make a hand" speaks to the value of a rich our-o-logue.

Each chapter begins with a question that guides the chapter and is followed by a case example to illuminate the chapter concepts. In addition, the body of each chapter includes written reflection spaces for two audiences: an individual reader and a group of readers, such as professional learning communities, book groups, and students in a college classroom. The intent of these reflection spaces is to enhance individual reflection and an our-o-logue for advancing student achievement in which all participants are considered rich and valuable resources. Many of the chapters conclude with suggestions for putting the ideas and strategies that are presented into practice.

Chapter 1: A Call for Reframing. The first chapter provides an in-depth discussion of the major federal initiatives that have attempted to close the achievement gap. It also provides a current overview of the gap and the need for an asset-based premise for addressing it. The chapter concludes with a reframe and a call for using asset-based language to enhance student achievement. An important aspect of this and subsequent chapters is its reflective prompts, which are used to extend our thinking (individually and collectively/collaboratively) about our work.

Chapter 2: Using a Four-Pronged Framework. This chapter provides a description of students who carry academic language as well as learners of academic language and introduces the four-pronged framework.

Chapter 3: Learning as a Sociocultural Process. This chapter describes how learning is a sociocultural process that must be tied to students' personal, cultural, and world knowledge. It also describes how learning must be compelling, meaningful, and relevant for students and provides a rationale for using cooperative learning (paired and group work) as a mainstay for enhancing academic language development.

Chapter 4: Learning as a Developmental Process. This chapter is devoted to the principles and practices of academic language and literacy learning, including a means for teachers and other stakeholders to use a model of explicit instruction that is based on academic literacy and rich vocabulary development.

Chapter 5: Learning as an Academic Process. Using a *backward design,* the formation of clear content and "do" objectives, and explicit vocabulary instruction/development, this chapter addresses academic language from a content literacy learning, curriculum standards–based perspective.

Chapter 6: Learning as a Cognitive Process. This chapter focuses on the development and enhancement of higher order thinking skills. It reinforces the importance of visualizing learning and understanding language functions and Bloom's taxonomy as a means for fostering student development of thinking-to-learn skills.

Chapter 7: Engaging in Parent Partnerships. Home–school engagement is a key contributor to student success and membership in the school community. This chapter draws from the four-pronged framework as it relates to parent engagement and uses an asset-based model to describe ways of actively engaging parents in their child's schooling.

Chapter 8: Making Data-Driven Decisions. This chapter provides a rationale, resources, and tools for using the four-pronged framework to strengthen student achievement and parent engagement.

1

A Call for Reframing

Why is it important to look closely at language and literacy to advance student achievement?

Let's begin our discussion of this question by visiting Jana Fielding's kindergarten classroom.

Jana Fielding teaches kindergarten at Main Street School, a culturally and linguistically diverse public school in an old industrial city in the Midwest. While most of her students are from homes where parents and guardians speak standard[1] American English, she has observed an increase in the number of students and families who don't. Though Mrs. Fielding has been teaching for 5 years and is a dedicated and committed teacher, she is constantly concerned about her capacity to meet the diverse needs of her students, particularly those who are commonly referred to as speakers of nonstandard English.[2]

Lily is a student in Mrs. Fielding's kindergarten class. Each day, Lily walks to school with her mother, and the two of them share the duty of pushing her 2-year-old brother in his stroller. The walk is filled with stories that her mother shares from her own childhood. These usually are a continuation of the bedtime stories that Lily's mother and father typically share with her about their families and childhoods. As they draw closer to Main Street School, Lily and her mother generally find it difficult to separate. The school's rule that they say goodbye to each other at the school's front door, as opposed to at the door of Lily's classroom, is hard for both of them, especially Lily's mother, who would prefer to leave her child directly in the care of Mrs. Fielding and ask informally about how her daughter is doing. To Lily's mother, this is a social exchange that she expected would occur. Instead, she receives written information from Mrs. Fielding, including "reading to your child," "nutrition for your child," "ways to help your child be ready for school," and more. Lily generally comes home with her backpack filled with these types of parent informational documents.

Lily's mother and father both work at a local hotel in the housekeeping department. Lily's mother works the 8:30 am–4:30 pm shift, and during the past year Lily's father has been working the evening and late-night shifts, typically logging 16-hour days so that his family can afford to continue living in their apartment. He is generally asleep when Lily wakes for and returns home from school, and she doesn't see much of him. Prior to dinner, Lily typically plays with her dolls and comes to the dinner table when her mother states, "It's time to eat. Wash your hands and come to the table." Lily's life outside of school is mostly spent at home with her parents and younger brother. On a regular basis, they meet with extended family members for family dinners and are active in their local church. Her parents are hopeful that Lily will achieve what they have not: a high school education. Both of them dropped out of school in their teens for similar reasons; they did not feel that school "was for them."

During the language arts block, Mrs. Fielding separates her class into groups and places Lily in the group that she believes needs extra support. Mrs. Fielding and Mrs. Talbot, a reading specialist, work with the class. Mrs. Talbot works with Lily's group on phonological and decoding skills, as she strongly believes that phonemic awareness and decoding skills are a primary need for these students. Much of what Mrs. Talbot does is drill-and-skill work using activity sheets to reinforce these concepts. While this is occurring, Mrs. Fielding works with another group, usually reading aloud from one of the stories that she has selected and working on comprehension skills. When Mrs. Fielding and Mrs. Talbot check in with each other about Lily, they begin to consider whether she should be tested for having a learning disability because of what they consider to be poor literacy development.

When Lily's parents do not come for the parent conference, Mrs. Fielding knows that they love their child, but she cannot think of anything that she can do to engage them beyond what is already occurring.

The following two reflection prompts have been separated for individual study and team study. Complete the prompt that applies to your particular context.

REFLECTION PROMPT FOR INDIVIDUAL STUDY

Time for Reflection:

Reflect on the following questions, and write a response.

- What suggestions do you have for helping Mrs. Fielding to engage Lily's parents?

- What additional information would you like to know about Lily? Why?

REFLECTION PROMPT FOR TEAM STUDY AND OUR-O-LOGUE

Time for Reflection:

Reflect on the following questions, write a response, and prepare to discuss it with your team.

- What suggestions do you have for teachers who work with students like Lily?

(Continued)

(Continued)

 • How would you envision enacting these suggestions?

Many educational scholars, practitioners, and others have written extensively about teaching students from underserved populations. This includes students who live below the poverty line (Books, 2004; Lindsey, Karns, & Myatt, 2010, Tileston & Darling, 2009), are from multicultural contexts (Davis, 2007; Delpit, 1995, 2011; Miramontes, Nadeau, & Commins, 2011; Nieto & Bode, 2012; Sylwester, 2003; Tomlinson, 2003), and are English learners (August & Shanahan, 2006; Haynes & Zacarian, 2010; Zacarian, 2011). It also reflects working with diverse families (Henderson, Mapp, Johnson, & Davies 2007; Lawrence-Lightfoot, 2004; Ogbu, 1978). Each provides solid information about how to work with students and families from these particular perspectives.

These contributions are made more relevant by the realities of an ever-increasing population of students and families living below the poverty line; the significant rate of chronic absenteeism among the nation's poor (Balfanz & Byrnes, 2012); and an increase in racial, ethnic, and linguistic diversity against the backdrop of educators who remain relatively the same—White and middle class (Hollins & Guzman, 2005; Zeichner & Hoeft, 1996). These changing demographics force us to think more carefully and deeply about how to meet the needs of diverse student and parent populations. However, thinking in this way is not new. At the national level, a variety of events and initiatives have intended to shape the education of American public school students. Some of these paid particular attention to underserved populations and closing the achievement gap. The next section centers on five particular time periods/ efforts: the civil rights movement of the 1960s, the charter school movement of the 1990s, the No Child Left Behind Act of 2001, the Race to the Top program that came along several years later, and the Common Core State Standards of 2010. These put into context some of the historic intiatives that have occurred to improve, among other areas, the education of the nation's students.

WHAT KEY HISTORICAL EVENTS HAVE SHAPED THE EDUCATION OF AMERICAN PUBLIC SCHOOL STUDENTS?

The Civil Rights Movement: An End to Separate but Equal

During the civil rights movement of the 1960s, the federal government commissioned the U.S. Department of Health, Education, and Welfare to conduct an assessment of students from diverse races, religions, and national origins for the purpose of evalutating their access and rights to an equal education. Known as the Coleman Study, it brought to light the inequalities that were occurring nationwide and the need to create more equal access to education, particularly for students from minority populations (Gamoran & Long, 2006). Since the 1960s, a multitude of studies have been conducted and a variety of initiatives enacted with the hope of closing the achievement gap between some minority student populations (e.g., students who are living in poverty, students learning English as a new language) and the dominant student population. It's important to look at a few of the major initiatives that shaped what we have come to call the rights of every child, including students from underserved populations, to receive access and opportunity to an education.

During the 1960s, the United States experienced what is commonly called the *civil rights movement.* The movement represented a mass protest against the racial segregation and discrimination practices occurring throughout the nation, and particularly in the southern states. Many renowned historians, educational scholars, and others believe that the movement took root after the Civil War in large part because of significant continued and pervasive practices of racism. It also came on the heels of one of the most seminal U.S. Supreme Court cases, *Brown v. Board of Education of Topeka, Kansas,* a 1954 case that overturned a post–Civil War precedent from *Plessy v. Ferguson,* which had allowed blacks to be separated from whites so long as they were given *separate but equal* rights and access to services, including education. The *Brown* decision overturned the 1896 precedent, ruling that separate was inherently unequal.

In 1964, the U.S. Congress passed a landmark law banning discrimination based on race, ethnicity, and gender. In 1967, President Lyndon Johnson sought a better way to end practices of racism, discrimination, and segregation. He implemented the Elementary and Secondary Education Act (ESEA), the first of its kind, requiring that any institution receiving federal funding could not deny anyone access to any program or activity based on race, color, or national origin (Hanna, 2005). It was part of what has been commonly referred to as Johnson's War on Poverty, the federal government's attempt to enact legislation that would bring about equal opportunities to underserved populations. A few years after ESEA was enacted, the federal government also passed the Bilingual Education Act to address the specific learning needs of linguistic minority students (Baker, 2006; Osorio-O'Dea, 2001). While many additional initiatives occurred during this time period, it is important to note that their focus was on equality of social justice and social benefits. Thirty years after the civil rights movement began, another movement arose, the charter school movement.

The Charter School Movement

In an attempt to improve children's educational outcomes, new legislation in the 1990s, with full support from President Bill Clinton, provided a public school option, known as public charter schools, for parents seeking alternative choices to traditional public education. According to the U.S. Department of State (n.d.) the purpose of charter schools is to do the following:

- Increase opportunities for learning and access to quality education for all students
- Create choice for parents and students within the public school system
- Provide a system of accountability for results in public education
- Encourage innovative teaching practices
- Create new professional opportunities for teachers
- Encourage community and parent involvement in public education
- Leverage improved public education broadly

In 1999, close to 400,000 students were enrolled in charter schools, and by 2011, they had become an even more popular choice, with over two million students enrolled in 41 states[3] that enacted laws approving of the public charter school option (National Alliance of the Public Charter Schools, 2011). As a result, in some areas the local public school became just one choice among many other options. For example, in a newspaper article aptly titled "A Daily Diaspora, a Scattered Street"

(Ebbert & Russell, 2011), we learn that 19 school-aged Boston-area children living on one city block attended 15 different public, public charter, and private schools. We might surmise, after reading this and other related articles, that charter schools are a better option than public schooling for the nation's students. The acclaimed documentary *Waiting for "Superman"* (Guggenheim, 2010) might affirm this perception. However, do charter schools yield any better student outcomes than do public schools? Research funded by the federal government indicates that most students do not fare any better in charter schools than they do in public school systems (Gleason, Clark, Tuttle, & Dowyer, 2010).

No Child Left Behind

While these initiatives were intended to remedy long-held practices of racism, discrimination, and prejudice, the outcomes reveal that achievement among underserved populations is significantly less than it is for White and Asian American students (Swanson, 2011). In an attempt to address this persistant problem, the No Child Left Behind Act of 2001 (NCLB) was signed into law by President George W. Bush as part of the reauthorization of ESEA. Its intent was to improve achievement for all students, particularly those who were struggling. The NCLB remedy called for setting new standards of accountability for results, greater flexibility in the use of school funding, more choice for parents from disadvantaged backgrounds, and an emphasis on teaching methods that have been scientifically proven to work (U.S. Department of Education, 2008). Hence, over a century after the country's first attempt to create equality, albeit initially based on the mistaken belief that separate could be equal, different means were enacted to better ensure that the needs of all students would be met.

Race to the Top, a Grant Initiative Targeted to Improvement

In 2009, President Barack Obama enacted the Race to the Top program, a new grant initiative under the American Recovery and Reinvestment Act, which

> encourage[s] and reward[s] States that implement significant reforms in the four eduation areas . . . : enhancing standards and assessments, improving the collection and use of data, increasing teacher effectiveness and achieving equity in teacher distribution, turning around struggling schools. (U.S. Department of Education, 2010, p. 3)

This grant initiative is targeted to remedy the dropout crisis by ensuring that all students have the opportunity not just to complete high school successfully, but to be properly prepared for college. Many believe that a degree in higher education is a primary need for our nation so that we may continue to prosper in the 21st century.

Common Core State Standards

The initiatives that we have discussed thus far were specifically targeted to close the achievement gap by better ensuring that underserved minority student populations (i.e., students living below the poverty line and students from diverse racial, cultural, ethnic, and linguistic backgrounds) would receive equal access to an appropriate education. In addition, an initiative by the National Governors Association and the Council of Chief State School Offices was developed in 2010: the Common Core State Standards. These are intended to provide a clear set of standards for English language arts and mathematics "to prepare our children for college and the workforce" (Common Core State Standards Initiative, 2012, para. 1), regardless of where in the country they live and attend school. At the time of this writing, 44 U.S. states had adopted the Common Core State Standards.

Where Are We Now?

A century and several major initiatives later, has the achievement gap experienced by groups of underserved students been closed? While the Common Core State Standards have not been in effect long enough to know whether they will have a significant impact on this outcome, it is important to note that they do not call for a different approach to be used in the classroom. Rather, they call for a common set of outcomes for what it is students should know and be able to do. A look at what is occurring shines some light on this important question.

In a report released in June 2011, completed by the Editorial Project in Education Research Center and using the most current available data on high school graduates, we learn that the graduation rates of America's public and public charter school students are going up (Swanson, 2011). The United States boasted a graduation rate of 71.7% for the class of 2008, the highest since the 1980s. We should be proud of this accomplishment. However, when we disaggregate the data, we learn that underserved groups continue to be among the most underachieving and vulnerable or at-risk of failing to meet the Race to the Top standards that have been set. The same outcome can be said for the initiatives and federal legislation that preceded Race to the Top. America's most vulnerable populations continue to be underserved and have the poorest of outcomes.

With all of this light being shone on federal initiatives and the charter school movement, what are we learning? At a fundamental level, certain groups of students continue to do poorly.

Perhaps, six decades after the civil rights movement is not a long enough period of time for our nation to move beyond the hundreds of years of slavery, suppression, and oppression that preceded it. While this is an important reality to understand, these outcomes do reflect an urgent need to look more closely at the ways that we are educating underserved populations. A broader lens is needed for us to understand what occurred historically so that we can consider what is needed to advance achievement for all students.

WHAT ARE THE MAJOR CHARACTERISTICS OF STUDENTS WHO ARE DOING POORLY IN U.S. SCHOOLS?

From the previously mentioned report about the current graduation rates of students, we learn the following:

> Although the rates for key historically underserved groups have improved over time, they remain a cause for concern. Among Latinos in the class of 2008, 58 percent finished high school with a diploma, while 57 percent of African-Americans and 54 percent of Native Americans graduated. On average, 68 percent of male students earn a diploma compared with 75 percent of female students, a 7-percentage-point gender gap that has remained virtually unchanged for years. High school completion rates for minority males consistently fall near or below the 50 percent mark. Suburban districts graduate considerably more students on average than do those serving urban communities, 76 percent vs. 64 percent. Regardless of location, graduation rates in districts characterized by heightened levels of poverty or racial or socioeconomic segregation fall well below the national average, typically ranging from 58 percent to 63 percent. (Swanson, 2011)

Figure 1.1 provides a graphic description of the proportion of students who are graduating from high school.

Figure 1.1   Graduation Rates (%) on the Rebound

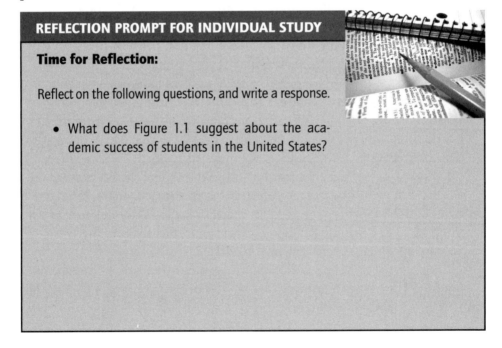

Source: Swanson, Christopher. As first appeared in Education Week, June 9, 2011. Reprinted with permission from Editorial Projects in Education.

The following two reflection prompts have been separated for individual study and team study. Complete the prompt that applies to your particular context.

REFLECTION PROMPT FOR INDIVIDUAL STUDY

Time for Reflection:

Reflect on the following questions, and write a response.

- What does Figure 1.1 suggest about the academic success of students in the United States?

- What are the key factors that you believe might explain these results?

**REFLECTION PROMPT FOR TEAM
STUDY AND OUR-O-LOGUE**

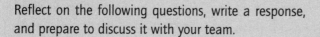

Time for Reflection:

Reflect on the following questions, write a response,
and prepare to discuss it with your team.

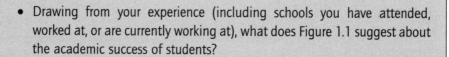

- Drawing from your experience (including schools you have attended, worked at, or are currently working at), what does Figure 1.1 suggest about the academic success of students?

- What key factors do you believe might explain these results?

While it is critical to understand racial, economic, and gender differences, a closer look at language and literacy, especially the type of language and literacy that are needed to perform successfully in school, is an important key to unlocking more effective ways for closing the achievement gap. In the United States, along with 350 different languages spoken among the nation's English learners (Garcia, Jensen, & Scribner, 2009) many dialects are spoken. While African American Vernacular English is the most widely studied of the dialects of English spoken in America, according to Labov (2006) many other dialects are also used by our nation's students, including Latin American Vernacular English, Alaskan American Vernacular English, Hawaiin American Vernacular English, and Indigenous American Vernacular English. There are also regional dialect differences. In addition, each dialect has its own code (Delpit, 1995). In African American Vernacular English, for example, the invariant form of the verb *be* is commonplace and, according to Labov, began to take root during the early 1900s or earlier. Labov offers the following examples of this type of usage of the verb *be:*

She be here (p. 7).

When I be asking my mom for money (p. 7).

I know they be lyin (p. 7).

This is not to say that dialects do not change. Like any language system, they are dynamic and evolve with the culture and context in which they occur, making communication more rich and descriptive. As a result, students come to school using dialects and languages that reflect their home cultures, and their language systems are richly diverse. However, the U.S. educational system does not seem to place much value on languages other than academic language. Indeed, academic language is *the* language that has what Delpit (1995) calls the "culture of power" (p. 24). Why is this so important? Let's take a closer look at the teaching profession.

Literacy Framework of Academic Language Carriers and Academic Language Learners

As educators, we want students to use academic language. What is academic language? To look at this more closely, it is helpful to understand what it means to be a proficient user of or communicatively competent in academic language. The federal definition of an English learner sheds some light on what is needed for a student to be a proficient user of academic language in school. This includes the following:

(i) the ability to meet the state's proficient level of achievement on state assessments

(ii) the ability to successfully achieve in classrooms where the language of instruction is English

(iii) the opportunity to participate fully in society (U.S. Department of Education, 2004)

An important characteristic of the federal definition is that a student must be able "to meet the state's *proficient* level of achievement on State assessments." While these may vary from state to state, the common requirement is that a student have the ability to use academic language and that this usage is needed to participate fully in society. Referring back to Labov's (2006) example, let's look at a classroom interaction that occurs in Mrs. Fielding's kindergarten classroom, from the case example at the beginning of this chapter. In this exchange, Mrs. Fielding asks Lily a question.

Mrs. Fielding: Lily, do you have the persmission slip for the class trip?

Lily: It be at home.

In this short exchange, what do we note about Lily's speech and its relation to academic language? Namely, that Lily does not speak academic language. Not surprisingly, we might also find ourselves using deficit-based language to describe the differences between the language that Lily uses and the language that her peers use, including the language that I have used thus far. Common deficit-based descriptors include terms such as *non-literacy-oriented* and *nonstandard speaker.* This is particularly relevant for American educational systems. Why? Across the country, rural, suburban, and urban schools are becoming more populated by speakers of nonstandard English as well as English learners (Calderon & Minaye-Rowe, 2010; Zacarian, 2011). While the highest concentrations are in urban areas, rural and suburaban communities are rapidly finding themselves teaching students who do not carry academic language into school. Indeed, many academic language learners struggle greatly to become proficient in English, and there is growing concern about this issue (Calderon & Minaye-Rowe, 2010).

Addressing this situation calls for a state of emergency to transform our educational system and for reframing our understanding about the students we teach. Specifically, we need to understand that achievement is directly related to the students who carry academic language and that underachievement is directly related to a large and growing number of students who are academic language learners.

An important distinction should be made here about what is meant by *academic language* and *carriers* versus *learners*. Jeffrey Zwiers (2008) provides a helpful definition of academic language. He says that all students

> start with a foundation of language that has been building from early childhood. This foundation represents the language and thinking of family, home culture, and community. During the school years a student builds up other levels of general and specialized language from this foundation. An important layer is the general academic language of thinking and literacy that is used across the disciplines. (p. 2)

Central to Zwiers's (2008) definition is that academic language is built from the *foundation* of a child's language and continues to build both broadly and specifically from this core. Some children come to school with academic language readiness skills that include a high level of foundational language. That is, they carry these into school at the earliest ages and continue to develop their academic language in home and in school. In this book, these students are referred to as those who *carry academic language.* These are students who come to school with the type of language that Zwiers refers to as foundational. Further, whether they enter as kindergartners or as seniors in high school, they have the foundational and academic language that is needed to learn in general and subject-specific ways to communicate successfully in a school setting.

In contrast, *learners of academic language* are students who must learn this level of language while they are also learning general and subject-specific language to communicate successfully in school. Here is another way of looking at the issue: Students who carry academic language have already *cracked the code* (Wells, 1994) for using what we commonly refer to as *school language.*

A closer look at the two groups is helpful, so in Chapter 2 we will explore the differences between them. We will learn that language differences, in relation to these two groups, reflect more than language, and we will begin exploring the four-pronged framework for advancing student achievement through the learning of academic language. We will also discuss the need for looking at this issue through a collaborative lens, which I refer to as an *our-o-logue*—a way for students, parents, teachers, leaders, community members, and others to collaborate to build successful schools. Before moving on to Chapter 2, however, it's important to take a few moments to reflect on what we have discussed in this chapter.

The following two reflection prompts have been separated for individual study and team study. Complete the prompt that applies to your particular context.

REFLECTION PROMPT FOR INDIVIDUAL STUDY

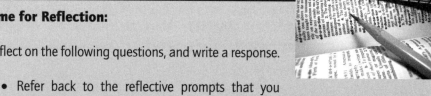

Time for Reflection:

Reflect on the following questions, and write a response.

- Refer back to the reflective prompts that you have responded to in this chapter. Analyze your responses in terms of any deficit-laden language about students.

- What do you believe is needed for Lily's teacher to match Lily's strengths and background?

REFLECTION PROMPT FOR TEAM STUDY AND OUR-O-LOGUE

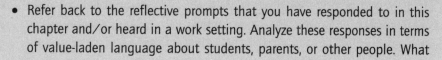

Time for Reflection:

Reflect on the following questions, write a response, and prepare to discuss it with your team.

- Refer back to the reflective prompts that you have responded to in this chapter and/or heard in a work setting. Analyze these responses in terms of value-laden language about students, parents, or other people. What

(Continued)

(Continued)

> are some ways of addressing this language so that it is affirmational or positively focused and not value laden?

- What suggestions might you have for helping others refocus their perceptions so that this can be a collaborative effort?

Here are some important thoughts to consider before moving on to the next chapter. There is a good chance that we as teachers come from different backgrounds and experiences than do some of our students. Indeed, most of the nation's students are taught by White, middle-class teachers (Hollins & Guzman, 2005; Zeichner & Hoeft, 1996). In addition, we are generally prepared to teach by educators who are primarily "white middle class females, from suburbs and small towns and have limited experience with people from cultures other than their own" (Hollins & Guzman, 2005, p. 485). Indeed, in a meta-analysis of 101 teacher preparation studies, Hollins and Guzman (2005) found that most preservice teachers were more comfortable and preferred working with students and parents from backgrounds similar to their own. This is particularly relevant. Why? Most educators carry academic language as an important part of their identity. Further, most colleges do not require their students to learn about teaching diverse populations. Courses in key areas about diversity and heterogeneity are more likely to be optional electives (Ladson-Billings, 1995). Thus, while America's population of academic language learners is increasing rapidly, most of us have no training and/or experience working with these learners. The subsequent chapters of this book are intended to extend our collaborative thinking and practice with the goal of advancing student achievement.

SUMMARY

In this chapter, we discussed some of the key historic movements and initiatives that were intended to improve the education of the nation's public and public charter school students. Included in this discussion were the civil rights movement and the charter school movement; two key regulatory acts, the Elementary and Secondary Education Act and the No Child Left Behind Act; the Race to the Top grant initiative; and, most recently, the Common Core State Standards, an initiative led by many of the country's governors. We also discussed some of the major characteristics of students who are chronically doing poorly despite the initiatives that have been targeted for improvement as well as the general teaching population who remain primarily White, middle class, and monolingual English speaking, with little to no training with students who are different from themselves. We began to reframe the achievement gap as being between students who carry academic language and students who are learning academic language.

REFERENCES

August, D., & Shanahan, T. (2006). *Developing literacy in second-language learners.* Mahwah, NJ: Lawrence Erlbaum.

Baker, C. (2006). *Foundations of bilingual education and bilingualism* (4th ed.). Tonawanda, NY: Multilingual Matters.

Balfanz, R., & Byrnes, V. (2012). *Chronic absenteeism: Summarizing what we know from nationally available data.* Baltimore, MD: Johns Hopkins University, Center for Social Organization of Schools.

Books, S. (2004). *Poverty and schooling in the U.S.: Contexts and consequences.* Mahwah, NJ: Lawrence Earlbaum.

Calderon, M. E., & Minaya-Rowe, L. (2010). *Preventing long-term ELs: Transforming schools to meet core standards.* Thousand Oaks, CA: Corwin.

Common Core State Standards Initiative. (2012). *About the standards.* Retrieved from http://www.corestandards.org/about-the-standards

Cummins, J. (1979). Cogitive/academic language proficiency, linguistic interdependence, the optimum age question and some other matters. *Working Papers on Bilingualism, 19,* 121–129.

Davis, B. M. (2007). *How to teach students who don't look like you: Culturally relevant teaching strategies.* Thousand Oaks, CA: Corwin.

Delpit, L. (1995). *Other people's children: Cultural conflict in the classroom.* New York, NY: New Press.

Delpit, L. (2011). *"Multiplication is for white people": Raising expectations for other people's children.* New York, NY: New Press.

Ebbert, S., & Russell, J. (2011, June 12). A daily diaspora, a scattered street. *The Boston Sunday Globe*, p. 1.

Freeman, Y., & Freeman, D. E. (2002). *Closing the achievement gap: How to reach limited-formal-schooling and long-term English learners.* Portsmouth, NH: Heinemann.

Gamoran, A., & Long, D. A. (2006). *Equality of educational opportunity: A 40-year retrospective.* Madison: University of Wisconsin-Madison, Wisconsin Center for Educational Research. Retrieved from http://www.wcer.wisc.edu/publications/workingPapers/Working_Paper_No_2006_09.pdf

Garcia, E. E., Jensen, B. T., & Scribner, K. P. (2009). The demographic imperative. *Supporting English Language Learners, 66*(7), 8–13.

Gleason, P., Clark, M., Tuttle, C. C., & Dwoyer, E. (2010). *The evaluation of charter school impacts.* Retrieved from http://www.mathematica-mpr.com/publications/pdfs/education/charter_school_impacts.pdf

Guggenheim, D. (Director). (2010). *Waiting for "Superman"* [Motion picture]. United States: Paramount Pictures Entertainment.

Hanna, J. (2005). *The Elementary and Secondary Education Act: 40 years later.* Retrieved from http://www.gse.harvard.edu/news_events/features/2005/08/esea 0819.html

Haynes, J., & Zacarian, D. (2010). *Teaching English langauge learners across the content areas.* Alexandria, VA: Association for Supervision and Curriculum Development.

Henderson, A. T., Mapp, K. L., Johnson, V. R., & Davies, D. (2007). *Beyond the bake sale: The essential guide to family-school partnerships.* New York, NY: New Press.

Hollins, E., & Guzman, M. T. (2005). Research on preparing teachers for diverse populations. In M. Cochran & K. M. Zeichner (Eds.), *Studying teacher education: The report of the AERA Panel on Research and Teacher Education* (pp. 477–548). Mahwah, NJ: Lawrence Erlbaum.

Labov, W. (2006). *Unendangered dialects, endangered people.* Retrieved from http://www.ling.upenn.edu/~wlabov/Papers/UDEP.pdf

Ladson-Billings, G. (1995). Multicultural teacher education: Research, practice, and policy. In J. A. Banks & C. A. McGee Banks (Eds.), *Handbook of research on multicultural education* (pp. 747–761). New York, NY: Macmillan.

Lawrence-Lightfoot, S. (2004). *The essential conversation: What parents and teachers can learn from each other.* New York, NY: Random House.

Lindsey, R. B., Karnes, M. S., & Myatt, K. (2010). *Culturally proficient education: An asset-based response to conditions of poverty.* Thousand Oaks, CA: Corwin.

Miramontes, O. B., Nadeau, A., & Commins, N. I. (2011). *Restructuring schools for linguistic diversity: Linking decision making to effective programs* (2nd ed.). New York, NY: Teachers College Press.

National Alliance of the Public Charter Schools. (2011). *Students overview.* Retrieved from http://dashboard.publiccharters.org/dashboard/students/page/overview/year/2011

National Alliance of the Public Charter Schools. (2012). *Find a charter school.* Retrieved from http://dashboard.publiccharters.org/dashboard/select/year/2012

Nieto, S., & Bode, P. (2012). *Affirming diversity: The sociopolitical context of multicultural education* (6th ed.).New York, NY: Pearson.

Ogbu, J. U. (1978). *Minority education and caste: The American system of cross-cultural perspective*. New York, NY: Harcourt Brace Jovanovich.

Osorio-O'Dea, P. (2001). *Bilingual education: An overview*. Retrieved from http://www.policyalmanac.org/education/archive/bilingual.pdf

Swanson, C. B. (2011). Analysis finds graduation rates moving up. Diplomas count: Beyond high school, before baccalaureate. *Education Week, 30*(34), 23–29.

Sylwester, R. (2003). *A biological bain in a cultural classroom: Applying biological research to classroom management*. Thousand Oaks, CA: Sage.

Tileston, D. W., & Darling, S. K. (2009). *Closing the poverty and culture gap: Strategies to reach every student*. Thousand Oaks, CA: Corwin.

Tomlinson, C. A. (2003). *Fulfilling the promise of the differentiated classroom*. Alexandria, VA: Association for Supervision and Curriculum Development.

U.S. Department of Education. (2004). *ESEA: Section 9101(25)*. Retrieved from http://www2.ed.gov/policy/elsec/leg/esea02/pg107.html

U.S. Department of Education. (2008). Title III of the Elementary and Secondary Education Act of 2001. *Federal Register, 73*, 61828–61844. Retrieved from http://www2.ed.gov/legislation/FedRegister/other/2008–4/101708a.pdf

U.S. Department of Education. (2010). *Race to the Top program: Guidance and frequently asked questions*. Retrieved from http://www2.ed.gov/programs/racetothetop/faq.pdf

U.S. Department of State. (n.d.). *U.S. charter schools: An overview and history of charter schools*. Retrieved from http://usinfo.org/enus/education/overview/charter_schools_history.html

Wells, G. (1994). The complementary contributions of Halliday and Vygotsky to a "language-based theory of learning." *Linguistics and Education, 6*, 41–90.

Zacarian, D. (2011). *Transforming schools for English learners: A comprehensive framework for school leaders*. Thousand Oaks, CA: Corwin.

Zeichner, K., & Hoeft, K. (1996). Teacher socialization for cultural diversity. In J. Sikula, T. Buttery, & E. Guyton (Eds.), *Handbook on research on teacher education* (2nd ed., pp. 525–547). New York, NY: Macmillan.

Zwiers, J. (2007). *Building academic language: Essential practices for content classrooms, grades 5–12*. San Francisco, CA: Jossey-Bass.

Zwiers, J. (2008). *We are all language teachers: Developing academic language in every lesson*. Retrieved from http://www.sccoe.k12.ca.us/depts/ell/6thacademicsuccess/Session%20XIII%20Handout.pdf

ENDNOTES

1. Various terms and phrases are used to describe students and families who possess school-matched language. These include users of *academic language* and *mainstream English* (Zwiers, 2007); *standard English* (Delpit, 1995; Freeman & Freeman, 2002) as well as students who possess *cognitive academic language proficiency* (Cummins, 1979). In this book, the term used to describe those who come to school with school-matched language skills is *students who carry academic language* because they carry these language skills with them into the classroom and

have the language readiness skills that they need in order to learn. In addition, the term used to refer to parents who possess these skills is *users of academic language*.

2. The term *nonstandard* is often used to describe students and families who do not possess school-matched language (Calderon & Minaya-Rowe, 2010; Delpit, 1995; Freeman & Freeman, 2009).

3. States approving charter schools include Alaska, Arizona, Arkansas, California, Colorado, Connecticut, Delaware, Florida, Georgia, Hawaii, Idaho, Illinois, Indiana, Iowa, Kansas, Louisiana, Maryland, Massachusetts, Michigan, Minnesota, Mississippi, Missouri, Nevada, New Hampshire, New Jersey, New Mexico, New York, North Carolina, Ohio, Oklahoma, Oregon, Pennsylvania, Rhode Island, South Carolina, Tennessee, Texas, Utah, Virginia, Wisconsin, and Wyoming, as well as the District of Columbia and Puerto Rico (National Alliance of the Public Charter Schools, 2012).

2 Using a Four-Pronged Framework

Why is it important to understand the difference between students who carry academic language and those who are learning it?

In Chapter 1, we were introduced to Jana Fielding's kindergarten classroom and one of her students, Lily, who does not possess the language skills that she needs to perform successfully in school. We begin this chapter by continuing our discussion of students who are learning academic language and students who carry it to and from school. Let's revisit Lily and then meet Thomas, a student who carries academic language into kindergarten.

We learned in Chapter 1 that Lily was not doing well in school and that Mrs. Fielding had placed her in the language arts group that she believed would provide Lily with the supports that she needed for improvement. We also learned that Mrs. Fielding would like to be a more effective teacher for students like Lily and work more closely with their parents; however, she is not sure what steps to take.

Thomas is also a student in Mrs. Fielding's class. During morning meeting, when Mrs. Fielding routinely introduces her students to the day's schedule, Thomas listens attentively and is often the first to raise his hand in response to her inquiries about the letters, sounds, and words that she references on the chart paper that sits on an easel adjacent to her seat. Thomas loves sounding out the words and, more often than not, making connections between what he already knows and what is written. He is well on his way to being a reader. During the parent conference, Mrs. Fielding lets his parents know how proud she is of his efforts and how well he is doing in class.

The following two reflection prompts have been separated for individual study and team study. Complete the prompt that applies to your particular context.

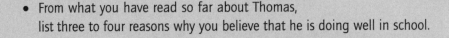

REFLECTION PROMPT FOR INDIVIDUAL STUDY

Time for Reflection:

Reflect on the following question, and write a response.

- From what you have read so far about Thomas,
  list three to four reasons why you believe that he is doing well in school.

**REFLECTION PROMPT FOR TEAM
STUDY AND OUR-O-LOGUE**

Time for Reflection:

Reflect on the following questions, write a response,
and prepare to discuss it with your team.

- Would you continue to place Thomas and Lily in different language arts
  groups? Explain your reasons for or against placing them in the same group.

- If you chose to place them together, how would you attend to both of their learning needs?

- If you chose to place them together, how would you ensure that Lily is seen as a rich and valuable reading resource?

Like Lily's parents, Thomas's parents are both employed. His mother works as a department store salesperson. His father works in the same hotel as Lily's father. He works in the business department, where he uses his accounting degree. When he arrives home from work, he likes to read the newspaper at the kitchen table while his wife prepares dinner. She generally relies on selecting her meal choices from her favorite magazine, *Cook's Illustrated*, and commonly uses it to guide her dinner preparation. While these routines are occurring, Thomas sits with his dad or walks in and out of the kitchen and in the process observes their behaviors. When the meal is ready to be eaten, one of his parents frequently states, "Dinner is ready. What do we do before we eat?" This question is really a directive for Thomas to wash his hands before coming to the dinner table to eat. During the fall Thomas plays soccer, in the winter he plays basketball, and in the spring and summer he plays T-ball. These are all part of the city's recreation department's activities. On rainy days, Thomas's mother brings him to the local library where he borrows as many books as he can carry about his favorite interest, dinosaurs. He also likes *Berenstain Bear* books, a favorite of his mother's when she was a young child. At bedtime, Thomas begs one of his parents to read to him. His mother affectionately notes that Thomas "drives her crazy" when he asks to be read the same story "over and over again."

So we have two students, Lily and Thomas, who are students in Mrs. Fielding's kindergarten class.

The following reflection prompts have been separated for individual study and team study. Complete the prompt that applies to your particular context.

REFLECTION PROMPT FOR INDIVIDUAL STUDY

Time for Reflection:

Reflect on the following questions, and write responses.

- What ideas come to mind about Lily's and Thomas's prospects for school success?

- What qualities of school readiness do you think are important? Why?

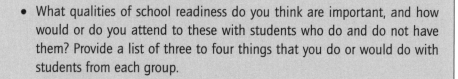

**REFLECTION PROMPT FOR TEAM
STUDY AND OUR-O-LOGUE**

Time for Reflection:

Reflect on the following question, write a response,
and prepare to discuss it with your team.

- What qualities of school readiness do you think are important, and how
  would or do you attend to these with students who do and do not have
  them? Provide a list of three to four things that you do or would do with
  students from each group.

Let's take a closer look at Lily and Thomas. In Chapter 1, we learned that Lily's parents did not graduate from high school and did not see value in school. In addition, we learned that Lily's parents tell her stories about their family histories and childhoods. In school, Lily is performing poorly. Mrs. Fielding is concerned that her language skills are well below where they should be, and she is thinking of referring Lily for a special education evaluation. Thomas's parents went to college, his father works as an accountant, and his mother works as a salesperson. Reading is commonplace in his home, and Thomas participates throughout the year in many sports activities as part of the city's recreational programming. Mrs. Fielding is pleased with Thomas's performance in school and is observing him starting to read.

STUDENTS WHO ARE CARRYING VERSUS STUDENTS WHO ARE LEARNING ACADEMIC LANGUAGE

Let's look more closely at which language practices enacted at home more closely parallel the language and literacy practices at school. To do this, let's assign Thomas the category of *carries academic language* and Lily, *academic language learner*. I developed the term *carries academic language* to refer to students who come to school with school-matched language skills.

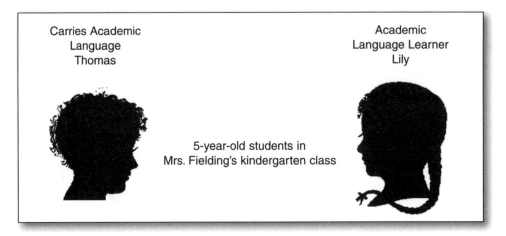

Figure 2.1   Carrying Versus Learning Academic Language

Carries Academic
Language
Thomas

Academic
Language Learner
Lily

5-year-old students in
Mrs. Fielding's kindergarten class

Carries Academic Language

How we describe different groups of students is often our means for framing their education. For example, Thomas routinely observes his father's daily practice of reading the newspaper and his mother's practice of reading recipes, magazines, books, and other printed materials. These behaviors lead to literacy development, and they cement reading as an essential behavior. In a great sense, Thomas's personal, world, cultural, and literacy knowledge is being bolstered by these literacy practices (Pransky, 2008; Rogoff, 1990; Zacarian, 2011; Zacarian & Haynes, 2012). In addition, Thomas's parents are college educated. If we combine the two characteristics, parents' education and exposure to literacy practices at a young age, we might surmise that his parents' behaviors are geared for Thomas to develop literacy skills and that education is important for his growth and development. In addition, it is clear that before Thomas set foot into an educational system, he had been exposed to the ever-present culture of reading and literacy development as a way of being and acting.

Thomas's parents also speak in ways that match what Delpit (1995) refers to as *middle-class speech*. For example, their expectation is that Thomas will know to wash his hands when preparing for the evening meal. Their question, "What do we do before we eat?" though a veiled directive, requires Thomas to engage in three separate sequentially ordered events. First, he will stop doing what he is doing; second, he will wash his hands; and third, he will come to dinner. These, too, are literacy-oriented behaviors in that they call for Thomas to sequence an event in a particular order, an activity that we as educators associate with an important thinking skill. Delpit notes these behaviors in a very different but important way. Lily's and Thomas's parents use language in ways that reflect their cultures. However, only Thomas's parents use it in the way that it is used in school. The middle-class speech that he is hearing and using at home parallels that of school. When Mrs. Fielding asks questions, for example, "Are we ready to line up?" he understands it properly as three messages: stop doing what he is doing, line up with his peers, and get ready for a transition. Thus, Thomas carries the language that he is learning at home into school and vice versa. In this sense, the two are matched and build from each other. Figure 2.2 reflects the behaviors that are commonplace among students who carry academic language.

The following reflection prompts have been separated for individual study and team study. Complete the prompt that applies to your particular context.

REFLECTION PROMPT FOR INDIVIDUAL STUDY

Time for Reflection:

Reflect on the following question, and write a response.

- As you read the bulleted list in Figure 2.2, think of how these do or do not associate with the practices that are needed for being successful in school, and note your ideas.

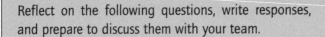

**REFLECTION PROMPT FOR TEAM
STUDY AND OUR-O-LOGUE**

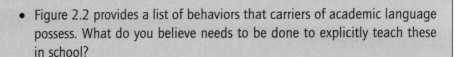

Time for Reflection:

Reflect on the following questions, write responses,
and prepare to discuss them with your team.

- Figure 2.2 provides a list of behaviors that carriers of academic language possess. What do you believe needs to be done to explicitly teach these in school?

- How might this be part of a systemic effort?

- What are two to three obstacles for enacting these? How would you address them?

Figure 2.2 Carries Academic Language

Thomas

Early and continuous exposure to

- rich vocabulary
- literacy as a cultural way of being and acting
- activities requiring organizational, problem-solving, and decision-making skills that match what is done in school
- what it means to be a learner
- the ability to generalize from the specific
- dialect skills that are similar to language used in classrooms

Learning Academic Language

Lily's parents often share their childhood and life experiences with her. She knows a good deal about her family's history and background as well as their cultural traditions as a result of being routinely exposed to these narrative storytelling activities. When she is with other family members, including her grandparents and others, they also engage in these types of behaviors. These are valuable behaviors that can be geared for literacy but do not necessarily match what occurs in school. That is, while much of Lily's personal, cultural, world, and language knowledge is rooted in these traditions, they do not reflect the practices that commonly occur in school. In addition, neither of Lily's parents completed high school, and they do not believe that school was for them.

This is not to say that Lily's parents do not care about her education. It is to say that her upbringing is quite different from Thomas's and that of other children reared in homes where parents provide their children with early literacy behaviors and routines that are like little suitcases ready to carry into school. First, Lily's parents are not as formally educated as Thomas's are. Second, their parenting, though loving and caring, is not geared for the development of literacy skills in the same way as many schools approach literacy. While we might mistakenly assume that they are not "good" parents because they are not gearing Lily for literacy, an alternate asset-based view is essential here. Lily's parents believe strongly in oral storytelling traditions. It is a critical interactional behavior, according to developmental psychologist Mary Gauvain (2001), and one that they use as part of Lily's development, understanding of the world around her, and, importantly, membership in their social community. If we think of this in terms of what Lily needs to be a member of her community, her parents are rearing her in the ways that will lead Lily to be successful in this regard (Gauvain, 2001). They are playing a key role in this developmental process. While parents are not the only ones involved in interacting with children, the types of interactions that parents and other adults have with children are part of their socialization process and are shaped around what is available and, of course, valued.

Cognitive development, according to Gauvain (2001), is dependent on the network and boundaries that are made available. As children are guided to participate in the world around them, such as playing sports and engaging in family discussions, or passively observing it, such as observing a church ritual, the more exposure they have, the broader their understanding becomes. Thus, the interactions (both passive through observation and active through participation) that children are routinely exposed to become the cement that holds their view of the world together. Let's look at this through the lenses of Lily and Thomas.

Lily spends most of her time at home with her immediate and extended family. She also attends church with her family. She is part of this close family network. Thomas participates on a weekly basis in the city's recreational sports programs. While both children are exposed to different people, the nature and scope of their social interactions are part of the network and boundaries of their development (Gauvain, 2001). All of these experiences provide opportunities that influence the children's developmental growth. In Lily's case, parenting is not focused on the types of literacy behaviors that are commonly nested in school. Further, the type of development that she is experiencing is also much more direct. As an example, she is told explicitly when to stop doing what she is doing, wash her hands, and come to dinner. If we are to view cognitive development as being influenced through what Rogoff (1990) defines as apprenticeships, Lily's development is being guided in a direct and explicit manner. For example, she is expected to be dependent on her mother's explicit directions.

It is important to connect the relationship between child development, school, and beyond—including the eventual workplace. If we are to connect how each relates to the other, we can begin to see how they are all related or not related to each other. To push this idea, let's first look at

Figure 2.3. It reflects the behaviors that are commonplace among people like Lily who are academic language learners.

Figure 2.3	Academic Language Learner

Early and continuous exposure to   Lily

- oral storytelling
- rich narrative of personhood and membership
- activities requiring following directions
- explicit direct parenting
- dialect that is distinct from school language
- vernacular speech

The following reflection prompts have been separated for individual study and team study. Complete the prompt that applies to your particular context.

REFLECTION PROMPT FOR INDIVIDUAL STUDY

Time for Reflection:

Reflect on the following question, and write a response.

- As you read the bulleted list in Figure 2.3, note how these do or do not associate with the practices that are needed for being successful in school.

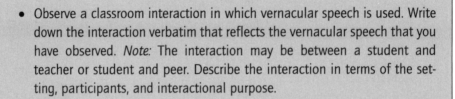

**REFLECTION PROMPT FOR TEAM
STUDY AND OUR-O-LOGUE**

Time for Reflection:

Reflect on the following tasks, write responses, and
prepare to discuss them with your team.

- Observe a classroom interaction in which vernacular speech is used. Write
  down the interaction verbatim that reflects the vernacular speech that you
  have observed. *Note:* The interaction may be between a student and
  teacher or student and peer. Describe the interaction in terms of the setting, participants, and interactional purpose.

- How does the speech event that you observed reflect the student's culture?
  List three to four reasons that you believe this is a reflection of culture.

Literacy activities are cultural activities (Rogoff, 1990). That is, they are
learned behaviors that occur through routine and continuous practice in a
social context. To be literate requires that we have engaged deeply in reading, writing, comparing, classifying, organizing, logic, and meaning-making
activities (Rogoff, 1990). Before children who carry academic language
begin kindergarten, they have already engaged in these activities for years.

Like Thomas, they have engaged in what Zwiers (2007b) calls *foundational* activities. In cultures where these foundational activities occur, for example, reading is a highly valued and practiced activity. This could not be more true for public and public charter school educators. Our profession is deeply rooted in literacy practices as a way of being and acting—they practically ooze out of our pores! However, the same cannot be said for all of our students, and herein lies the major distinction between educators and some students.

Let's look at the distinctions that have been made between students who carry academic language and students who are learning academic language. A primary difference is that parents of children who carry academic language are more educated. They typically have a college education and value literacy as a cultural way of being. They also have been exposed, and expose their children routinely, to rich vocabulary and activities that are matched with what will occur in school. In addition, they are generally speakers of or fluent in the dialect of school, the dialect that is needed to listen, speak, read, and write academically (Zwiers, 2007a). In this sense, regardless of the parents' home language (e.g., English, Spanish, Vietnamese), if they use academic language, they are likely to be raising their children to do the same.

Figure 2.4 lists the distinctions between users of academic language and academic language learners.

Figure 2.4

Academic Language User	Academic Language Learner
Early and continuous exposure to • rich vocabulary • literacy as a cultural way of being and acting • activities requiring organizational, problem-solving, and decision-making skills • what it means to be a learner • the ability to generalize from the specific • a dialect that matches school dialect	Early and continuous exposure to • oral storytelling • rich narrative of personhood and membership • activities requiring following directions • explicit direct parenting • a dialect that does not match school dialect • vernacular speech

The following reflection prompts have been separated for individual study and team study. Complete the prompt that applies to your particular context.

REFLECTION PROMPT FOR INDIVIDUAL STUDY

Time for Reflection:

Reflect on the following questions, and write responses.

- As you read the bulleted list in Figure 2.4, which student do you believe would be more successful in school? Why?

- What activities can you envision academic language learners performing well in school? How do these activities relate to what is needed to be successful in school?

REFLECTION PROMPT FOR TEAM STUDY AND OUR-O-LOGUE

Time for Reflection:

Reflect on the following tasks, write a response, and prepare to discuss it with your team.

- Observe a classroom setting in which a subject is being taught. Describe the lesson in detail is terms of what is evidenced from the Academic Language User column in Figure 2.4.

- Describe the lesson in detail is terms of what is evidenced from the Academic Language Learner column in Figure 2.4.

- What differences do you note between your response to the previous two tasks in terms of their applicability for students from each group?

THE CALL FOR A FOUR-PRONGED FRAMEWORK

At a foundational level, young children are exposed to early life experiences that are targeted for what is needed to be a member of the cultural group in which the children are being reared (Gauvain, 2001; Rogoff, 1990, 2003). Thus, children develop the language and communication skills that they need to actively participate in their home culture. For some, much of what has occurred and is occurring in their home culture is targeted for literacy development in a range of subject-specific areas such as as language arts, math, science, and social studies. This early exposure is what Zwiers (2007a, 2007b) refers to as the foundational building blocks of academic language. As children develop, their foundational level is expanded in both general and specific ways. In the field of education, we often refer to this as building from our students' background.

This concept is essential for us to consider as we develop ways for advancing student achievement. It also calls for a framework for understanding how to build on students' backgrounds, especially those who are learning academic language, so that they, too, can have meaningful access to learning and opportunities to be successful in school. To consider what it means to carry academic language means thinking more broadly about what is needed. Academic language is more than the ability to use words to listen, speak, read, and write.

To understand the concept of academic language, read the following excerpt and complete the reflection activity that follows it:

New Compact Microspectrometer Design Achieves High Resolution and Wide Bandwidth

Spectrometers have conventionally been expensive and bulky bench-top instruments used to detect and identify the molecules inside a sample by shining light on it and measuring different wavelengths of the emitted or absorbed light. Previous efforts toward miniaturizing spectrometers have reduced their size and cost, but these reductions have typically resulted in lower-resolution instruments. . . .

The 81-channel on-chip spectrometer designed by Georgia Tech engineers achieved 0.6-nanometer resolution over a spectral range of more than 50 nanometers with a footprint less than one square millimeter. The simple instrument—with its ultra-small footprint—can be integrated with other devices, including sensors, optoelectronics, microelectronics and microfluidic channels for use in biological, chemical, medical and pharmaceutical applications. (Adapted from Physorg.com, 2011)

The following reflection prompts have been separated for individual study and team study. Complete the prompt that applies to your particular context.

REFLECTION PROMPT FOR INDIVIDUAL STUDY

Time for Reflection:

Reflect on the following questions, and write responses.

- Summarize the excerpt in one or two sentences.

- What would you need to be a fluent user in the content of this excerpt?

REFLECTION PROMPT FOR TEAM STUDY AND OUR-O-LOGUE

Time for Reflection:

Reflect on the following tasks, write responses, and prepare to discuss them with your team.

- Complete the reflection task for individual readers listed above.

(Continued)

(Continued)

- With a partner, select a paragraph of text from a math, science, social studies, or language arts text. Summarize the excerpt in one or two sentences.

- Collaborate on a list of terms, words, idioms, and phrases (TWIPs) that you believe are key to know.

- Describe one concept that is being discussed in this paragraph, and discuss how it is dependent on the TWIPs that you identified in the previous question.

While there are only four sentences in this excerpt, each is packed with a special type of meaning that is indigenous to a certain group of people: electrical and computer science engineers. To understand this short passage well, we have to possess (1) depth of knowledge about the culture of electrical and computer science engineers; (2) the ability to listen, speak, read, and write in electrial and computer science language; (3) academic knowledge in this field of study to comprehend the text meaningfully and interact with it; and (4) the ability to use critical thinking skills about electrical and computer science in order to be able to contribute to it.

Being one who carries academic language requires the same type of proficiencies. Students must have sociocultural, linguistic, academic, and cognitive skill knowledge to perform academic tasks at any grade level. This does not occur naturally, however, for anyone. For some students, as we have discussed, their home language environment matches their school environment. Thus, what happens in school builds on the foundational academic language knowledge that has been and is occurring at home and vice versa. Thomas's parents are gearing their home culture to match what they believe will occur in Thomas's school; they are helping Thomas develop the skills that he needs to be a successful kindergarten student. Lily is being reared in a fine home culture as well; however, it is not focused on school culture in the same ways as Thomas's is. The absence of these connections is contributing to her doing poorly in school.

To address these differences more fully calls for a four-pronged framework (Collier, 1995; Zacarian, 2011) for planning and delivering high-quality learning experiences to students who carry academic language and, more important, those who are learning academic language so that we may better advance achievement for all students.

Four-Pronged Framework for a High-Quality Learning Environment

1. Learning is a sociocultural process. It involves building connections with students' "personal, social, cultural, and world experiences" (Zacarian, 2011, p. 77). While we often refer to this as building on students' backgrounds, it must be grounded in students' and their families' identities and personhood.

2. Learning is a developmental process. It calls for understanding the literacy proficiency level of each student and targeting instruction a little bit beyond it so that it is obtainable and reachable.

3. Learning is an academic process. It is "built on the prior learning experiences of students and when the academic language and learning goals are made explicit" (Zacarian, 2011, p. 78).

4. Learning is a cognitive process in which higher-order thinking skills are intentionally taught.

Each of these is interdependently connected and applies in all learning environments, especially in classrooms composed of diverse learners.

The following reflection prompts have been separated for individual study and team study. Complete the prompt that applies to your particular context.

REFLECTION PROMPT FOR INDIVIDUAL STUDY

Time for Reflection:

Reflect on the following question, and write a response.

- Write about the ways in which you infuse or would infuse each of the four prongs into your work. Write two to three specific ideas for each of the prongs.

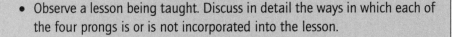

REFLECTION PROMPT FOR TEAM STUDY AND OUR-O-LOGUE

Time for Reflection:

Reflect on the following task, write a response to it, and prepare to discuss it with your team.

- Observe a lesson being taught. Discuss in detail the ways in which each of the four prongs is or is not incorporated into the lesson.

SUMMARY

In this chapter, we described the distinctions between students who carry academic language and students who are learning academic language. We drew from Rogoff (1990, 2003) and Gauvain (2001) to describe the influence of cultural development on children's language practices. We also highlighted early exposure to academic language in our discussion of Zwiers's (2007a, 2007b) foundational language concepts. We introduced the four-pronged framework for understanding how to create high-quality classroom environments that support carriers of academic language and, most important, the learning of academic language—learning as a sociocultural, developmental, academic, and cognitive process.

In Chapter 3, we will look more closely at the first of the four prongs: learning as a sociocultural process and how it must be tied to students' personal, cultural, and world knowledge.

REFERENCES

Collier, V. (1995). Acquiring a second language for school. *Directions in Language Education, 1*(4). Retrieved from http://www.ncela.gwu.edu/files/rcd/BE020668/Acquiring_a_Second_Language__.pdf

Delpit, L. (1995). *Other people's children: Cultural conflict in the classroom.* New York, NY: New Press.

Gauvain, M. (2001). *The social context of cognitive development.* New York, NY: Guilford Press.

Physorg.com. (2011). *New compact microspectrometer design achieves high resolution and wide bandwidth.* Retrieved from http://www.physorg.com/news/2011-06-compact-microspectrometer-high-resolution-wide.html

Pransky, K. (2008). *Beneath the surface: The hidden realities of teaching culturally and linguistically diverse young learners K–6.* Portsmouth, NH: Heinemann.

Rogoff, B. (1990). *Apprenticeship in thinking: Cognitive development in social context.* New York, NY: Oxford University Press.

Rogoff, B. (2003). *The cultural nature of human development.* New York, NY: Oxford University Press.

Zacarian, D., & Haynes, J. (2012). *The essential guide for educating beginning English learners.* Thousand Oaks, CA: Corwin.

Zacarian, D. (2011). *Transforming schools for English learners: A comprehensive framework for school leaders.* Thousand Oaks, CA: Corwin.

Zwiers, J. (2007a). *Building academic language: Essential practices for content classrooms, grades 5–12.* San Francisco, CA: Jossey-Bass.

Zwiers, J. (2007b). *Dimensions and features of academic language.* Retrieved from http://www.jeffzwiers.com/jeffzwiers-com-new_003.htm

3 Learning as a Sociocultural Process

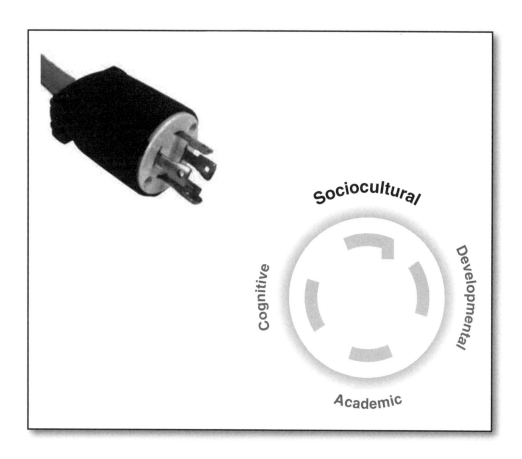

Why is a student's personal, cultural, and world knowledge important to learning academic language? Why is it also important to connect learning to issues that are socially relevant for students?

Let's begin this discussion by introducing Michael, a ninth-grade student who is an academic language learner.

Michael is a student in Mr. Franke's ninth-grade biology class. The class is studying a unit on genetics, and the biology course text includes a chapter on the scientific study of reproduction. Mr. Franke begins the unit by stating the day's learning objective. He tells his students, "Today, we will learn about gender probability followed by a preview of key vocabulary that will be included." He has taken time to review the text and select key terms, words, idioms, and phrases that his students will need to learn. These include *chromosomes, genes, DNA, RNA, sexual reproduction, zygote, X-chromosome,* and *Y-chromosome.* Mr. Franke has written these terms on the white board. Prior to class, he required his students to read the chapter on reproduction in their textbook and to jot down notes about what interested them. The lesson that he has planned for today's class includes a culminating activity of flipping coins to help his students understand the concepts of gender prediction. Let's have a look at his class.

Mr. Franke tells the class that they will be learning about genetic probability and determining the sex of a baby. After the class giggles quietly, Mr. Franke addresses the whole class with this question: "What do you know about probability and gender?" A few students raise their hands. They are the students who typically raise their hands in his class. They draw from the terms that are listed on the white board. Mr. Franke responds to them with his usual positive response: "Yes, good, and what else do we know?" When he is done calling on these students, he begins his "on the spot" callout to other students in class, including Michael. Michael responds to his query with "I don't know." Mr. Franke does not chastise or remark negatively to Michael. Rather, he continues to call on other students in class. As this is occurring, Mr. Franke responds to each student with "Good, what else do we want to add?" These Mr. Franke–student–Mr. Franke–student sequences occur for a period of time. During the exchanges, Michael jots down some notes, including "Gender Probly." He is not familiar with these two words or the term, and is having a hard time following the rapid student–teacher exchanges, but does not want to indicate to anyone, especially his peers, that he is having difficulties. He also found that he did not really understand the text that his class was assigned to read. There were too many terms to learn, and the explanations and photographs that were provided were not helpful to him. In short, he is not as able to grasp the concepts as comprehensively as some of his classmates.

In the next segment of the same class, Mr. Franke shows students two coins. He asks for a volunteer to label the coins. One side of one coin will be covered with an X, and the other with a Y. The second coin will be covered with an X on both sides. Michael does not volunteer to cover the coins. When Mr. Franke asks for a volunteer to flip the two coins and see where they land, Michael decides to volunteer and is selected. He hopes that Mr. Franke will see that he is trying to be a good student and hopes that his volunteerism is viewed positively. As he flips the coins, he sees that his first and second tosses include an XX combination and that his third results in an XY. He is not sure what these results mean. When Mr. Franke asks him about the results, he initially gives him a vacant look. Michael then looks to his classmates and the white board to see if there are any clues as to a response, and he doesn't see any. With the little information that he has written in his notes, he smiles and says, "Gender probly." Thinking that Michael understands the content, Mr. Franke smiles in response and then goes on to divide the class into pairs, furnishing each pair with two coins that they label with XX and XY, and engaging them in the coin toss activity. At the end of class, Mr. Franke reviews the day's objective and asks the students if they have met it. All respond in unison with, "Yes, Mr. Franke." However, the next day, when Michael is given a quiz about the meaning of gender probability, he leaves the section blank. He is not sure what he is being asked.

Let's look at another biology class. Mrs. Delgado is a ninth-grade biology teacher who is also teaching from the same course text. While she has preselected the same vocabulary, she has also secured a video about the birth of a baby called *Life's Greatest Miracle* (WGBH Educational Foundation, 1996–2012). The video depicts the life cycle of a baby from conception to birth. Mrs. Delgado decides to show the video to her students before they read the chapter and preview the vocabulary. On her white board, she writes, "How does life create life, including how do people create babies?" She introduces the unit by telling students that they are going to see a movie that was created for television and that taught her a lot about how babies are formed. "I never really thought much about what my body did inside my mother's body before I was born," she tells her class. She divides her class into pairs and asks each pair to describe what they think the movie will be about. "What do you think that you will see?" she asks her students.

"Now remember," she says, "it is a movie that actually depicts what a baby's life is like inside a mother during pregnancy. It is how life creates life, and it is amazingly a real movie that is about a real baby. With a partner, come up with five things that you think you will actually see when you watch this movie. Now, I am asking you to do this task. Here is one example that I think I will see in the movie. I think that babies look like babies from the beginning, so I think that I will see miniature babies with eyes, hands, feet, and so forth." As she says this, she points to a poster of a newborn baby that she has tacked to her classroom wall. "Now, I want you to enact the following roles with your partner: One partner must be the listener first, and the other the speaker, then rotate roles. Share five things that you think that you will see. Use your book, the photos that I have displayed on the class wall, and anything else that you think will help you in this task. You can point to pictures, passages in the book, or other supports that will help us see five different things that you think we will see in the movie." In this scenario, Michael is also a student in Mrs. Delgado's class.

The following reflection prompts have been separated for individual study and team study. Complete the prompt that applies to your particular context.

REFLECTION PROMPT FOR INDIVIDUAL STUDY

Time for Reflection:

Reflect on the following question, and write a response.

- Contrast the differences between Mr. Franke's and Mrs. Delgado's lessons.

- Do you believe that one is a more effective approach for academic language learners such as Michael? If yes, list three to four reasons why it is more effective.

**REFLECTION PROMPT FOR TEAM
STUDY AND OUR-O-LOGUE**

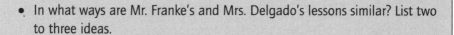

Time for Reflection:

Reflect on the following questions, write responses,
and prepare to discuss them with your team.

- In what ways are Mr. Franke's and Mrs. Delgado's lessons similar? List two to three ideas.

- In what ways are they different? Discuss three to four differences.

- Observe two classroom settings that are using the same curriculum (e.g., a second-grade mathematics class that is focused on the same standard and uses the same course text). This might include a class that you are teaching and a peer's. Discuss what is being done to pay attention to the academic language learners in these classes.

Each pair in Mrs. Delgado's class engages in the task. Some predict that they will see just what Mrs. Delgado thinks she will see, a miniature baby that will grow into a large baby and then will be born. Others predict that they will see the outside of a mother's "belly grow large" and that they will not see an actual baby until it is born. Others think that they will see a "blob that forms into a baby." Many are familiar with some of the vocabulary that Mrs. Delgado will be using. "We will be watching a movie about our DNA, about reproduction," some respond. Each pair shares their thoughts, and Mrs. Delgado notes these on the white board. They then spend the next segment of class watching the movie. When it is completed, Mrs. Delgado reviews with the class what they have watched. She connects what they discussed earlier in class with what they viewed in the movie. She then asks them to meet with their partner and discuss what they thought they would see versus what they actually saw. They share these differences with the whole class. At the end of the class period, Mrs. Delgado revisits the learning objective. Each student writes a short statement about what they learned and shares it with a partner. Mrs. Delgado tells them that they will be reading the chapter on the scientific study of reproduction later in the week.

She tells students that scientists have figured out a way to self-select whether they will have a girl baby or boy baby. For homework, she gives them the following task: "I would like you to discuss the following question with either a family member or a friend: Do you think that it is a good or bad thing for people to be able to select whether they will have a boy or girl baby? If you think it is good, why is it good? If it is a bad thing, why is it bad?" Mrs. Delgado writes the question on the white board and asks her students to copy the question in their notebooks. "Come to class tomorrow, and let's discuss our responses to this question," she says to her students as the end-of-class bell rings.

Let's have a closer look at the two scenarios. In the first one, Michael is in a class where his teacher, Mr. Franke, has taken the time to identify the key vocabulary that Michael and his classmates need to learn about the scientific study of reproduction. Mr. Franke has also prepared an activity, the coin toss, as a means to depict gender probability. He also has asked his students to prepare for this study by reviewing a chapter on this topic in their science text and jotting down things that interest them. Mr. Franke is trying hard to be a positive teacher, and he includes a variety of activities, including what he thinks will be a fun game, that he believes are targeted for his students to learn the content. However, while he is trying hard to be an effective and positive teacher, at least one of his students, Michael, is not able to learn successfully.

In the second scenario, Mrs. Delgado has also taken time to identify the key vocabulary that her students will need to learn the biology of reproduction. She has also prepared an activity that she believes will help to activate their prior knowledge and enhance their study of the biology text. Mrs. Delgado concludes the lesson by having them write a short statement about what they learned. Like Mr. Franke, she does this to have a means for knowing whether they have learned the content of the day's lesson. With all of these commonalities, however, there are fundamental distinctions between Mr. Franke's and Mrs. Delgado's lessons.

LEARNING BY BUILDING CONNECTIONS

Mrs. Delgado has figured out a way to help her students be invested in learning. She has done this by connecting the unit of study with their personal interests and knowledge (Vasquez, 2010; Zacarian, 2011a, 2011b). She builds connections between the biology content about reproduction and issues that are personal to her students' lives. Rather than focus on the course content through the course text, Mrs. Delgado secures a way to connect content to something that might be of interest to her students. She intentionally focuses on the language—the academic conceptual and conversational language that her students need–and its connection to their personal, cultural, and world experiences. She also is invested in capturing their interest in studying biology and helping them see value in learning so that they will be compelled to attend and stay in school (Balfanz & Byrnes, 2012). She does this because she knows the critical importance of hooking student interest and, more important, investment in learning. While many educators might think that learning must be connected to prior learning, it must first be connected to issues that are personal to students in order to help move academic content from being impersonal to personal (Zacarian, 2011b).

This is where the craft of teaching comes into play. While textbooks and other instructional materials may include activities that are intended to help spark student interest, we have to ask ourselves whether the activities that the text provides will really help our students be compelled to learn. Vasquez (2010) refers to this as our means for helping to rouse student interest in learning. A second and equally important element is that student investment must be maintained so that they can see value in it. We must do this by connecting the content that is to be learned with our students' personal, cultural, and world knowledge. This requires that we think carefully and creatively about building these important scaffolds to learning. Rather than do this alone, as many teachers do, an *our-o-logue* can be a very helpful means for collectively securing effective ways to spark student interest. Even the driest of curriculum can be made to come alive by creatively building personal connections to it in ways that are socially relevant for our students.

BUILDING SOCIALLY RELEVANT CONNECTIONS TO STUDENTS' LIVES

To engage in this important work, we must first consider sociocultural elements in planning and creating high-quality classroom, school, and parent engagement environments. Specifically, we need to identify what is relevant and compelling for our students in our teaching decisions as well as how we can help students and their families become invested in what is to be learned. Paulo Freire (1970) acknowledges this as our means for supporting student engagement. It is a critical way for framing learning as being personally and socially relevant to a student's life from a social justice perspective. It is our means for helping students consider social issues that are personally relevant to their lives. In Mrs. Delgado's class, for example, what would happen if all of her students think that it is good to be able to choose the gender of their babies and they all choose boy babies? What might happen to our world if this were to occur? This critical social question is an important means for hooking and investing student interest. Further, helping students see how what they are studying is related to social justice issues can greatly help in defining the teacher's role. Building connections that are socially relevant helps to connect content, in this case the scientific study of gender probability, to students' lives and cultures in ways that do more than draw from their prior academic and literacy backgrounds. This type of connection-making builds from students' personal, cultural, and world knowledge in ways that support their interest in the society in which they live and its connection to the content being studied. Connecting curriculum to issues that are relevant and personal to students' lives not only helps to spark student interest but also helps to keep them continuously invested in learning.

A fine example of this type of relevancy is Mrs. Baldwin's kindergarten science class. Drawing from the Massachusetts Department of Education's (2006) *Science and Technology/Engineering Curriculum Framework* section on Living Things and Their Environment, she is creating a science unit in which her students will engage in inquiry-based instruction through scientific exploration. Following the Skills of Inquiry, Experimentation, and Design section of the *Curriculum Framework,* Mrs. Baldwin knows that her lessons must do the following:

- Ask questions about objects, organisms, and events in the environment.
- Tell about why and what would happen if . . .
- Make predictions based on observed patterns.

- Name and use simple equipment and tools (e.g., rules, meter sticks, thermometers, hand lenses, balances) to gather data and extend the senses.
- Record observations and data with pictures, numbers, or written statements.
- Discuss observations with others.

But what Mrs. Baldwin teaches in terms of how she will engage students in this study involves thinking creatively. What does she do? She knows the importance of connecting the science unit to her students' personal lives. Many her students live in an apartment complex. It faces the back of the school, where there is a vernal pool that fills with water during the fall and spring months and freezes in the winter. Figure 3.1 is an example of a vernal pool.

The vernal pool behind the school has been slowly filling with trash, including a broken bicycle, cans, bottles, and old newspapers. Many of Mrs. Baldwin's students have told her about it, so she decides to create a yearlong science unit on the effects of pollution. She shows students the photo found Figure 3.1 and asks them if they have ever

Figure 3.1

seen such a pool of water. All of them respond about the pool behind their schoolyard.

In addition to studying the properties that would typically be found in the vernal pool, including frogs and other living things, Mrs. Baldwin divides the class into pairs and asks each pair to talk with another pair about their thoughts about the trash. As she walks among the small groups of students, she hears almost all of them respond that they don't like the trash. She helps her class think of ideas that they might have for making the vernal pool as pretty as the one in the photo. This leads to the students engaging in a "cleanup campaign." During the fall months, they enlist the school's students, staff, and parents, as well as community members, in cleaning the pool. While they are engaged in this effort, they also study the properties of a vernal pool. They observe the plants and animals that are indigenous to the area in and around it. The students not only engage in the inquiry-based science activities included in their state's curriculum framework, but they also engage in a powerful social justice activity that helps to improve their immediate environment. Mrs. Baldwin's students were very invested in this unit of study because it was personal and relevant to their lives.

The following reflection prompts have been separated for individual study and team study. Complete the prompt that applies to your particular context.

REFLECTION PROMPT FOR INDIVIDUAL STUDY

Time for Reflection:

Reflect on the following questions, and write responses.

- Mr. Silverstone, a second-grade teacher, is planning a unit of study on adding and subtracting numbers up to 100. What types of activities might he include to help connect this unit of study to his students' lives?

- Mrs. Ortiz, a middle school science teacher, is planning a unit of earth science study on tectonic plates. What types of activities might she include to help connect this unit of study to her students' lives?

- Mr. Crafts, a U.S. history high school teacher, is planning a unit of study on the Treaty of Versailles. What types of activities might he include to help connect this unit of study to his students' lives?

REFLECTION PROMPT FOR TEAM STUDY AND OUR-O-LOGUE

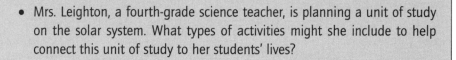

Time for Reflection:

Reflect on the following questions, write a response, and prepare to discuss it with your team.

- Mrs. Leighton, a fourth-grade science teacher, is planning a unit of study on the solar system. What types of activities might she include to help connect this unit of study to her students' lives?

(Continued)

(Continued)

- Select a math, science, or social studies topic that you teach or might teach that is connected to a standard (e.g., a state standard). With a partner, discuss how you might connect this topic with something that is socially relevant to your students' lives. Write your ideas for building these connections.

LEARNING AS AN INTERACTIVE SOCIAL PROCESS

Thus far, we have read about three different science teachers. Mr. Franke and Mrs. Delgado teach high school biology, and Mrs. Baldwin teaches kindergarten. Mrs. Delgado and Mrs. Baldwin engage their students in a large amount of paired and group work. For example, Mrs. Baldwin grouped pairs of her students together so that they filled the roles of observer and recorder. The pairs travel to the vernal pool on a weekly basis to note their observations. Why are she and Mrs. Delgado engaging in this method of teaching? Especially since many of their colleagues have told them that while paired and group work is nice, students often fall off task, and it is easier to do what Mr. Franke does, that is, keep the flow of conversation continuously directed through the teacher.

The small interactive space of paired and group work is an essential method for all educators. It provides an important time for students to practice using the language of content, or academic language, and to learn from peers (Cohen, 1994; Haynes & Zacarian, 2010; Zacarian, 2011b; Zacarian & Haynes 2012; Zwiers & Crawford, 2011). However, using paired and group work is no guarantee that students learn effectively. It requires many considerations.

First, it involves our willingness to reduce our authority in favor of a belief that students can and do learn effectively from and with each other (Cohen, 1994; Zacarian, 1996). Think of a classroom like Mr. Franke's. He is in control of all of the talk. It flows to and from him. Each exchange is between Mr. Franke and one of his students. While he asks open-ended questions, he asks them of the whole class and uses a method that requires individual students to respond to him. This teacher–student–teacher–student mode of interaction means that almost all of his students (with the exception of those who volunteer to speak or those he calls on) passively listen to the teacher–student exchanges. This type of classroom is one in which the majority of students are passive in the learning process.

Some teachers report that while they believe in the ideals of group work, it is often too difficult to manage, and they resort to a method like Mr. Franke's because it is their only way to ensure that the curriculum is covered. In an era of high-stakes tests in which teacher performance is being tied to student learning, it is understandable why teachers might feel pressured to be like Mr. Franke. Other teachers report that it is difficult for them to select groups because there are so many interpersonal dynamics among their students that are out of their control, and they cannot safeguard that any group will be effective. Indeed, group work is a complex method and endeavor that requires us to think deeply about it and plan carefully to enact it well (Zacarian, 1996, 2011a, 2011b). The following are some important considerations.

INDIVIDUALISTIC VERSUS COLLECTIVISTIC CULTURES

Some students come from cultures that are individualistic and others collectivistic. In individualistic cultures, independence is highly valued; independent thinking and choice are of primary concern to parents and families and the cultures in which children are being reared (DeCapua & Marshal, 2010; Hofstede, 2001; Hofstede & Hofstede, 2005; Zacarian & Haynes, 2012). U.S. dominant culture reflects this ideology, as do American public and public charter schools. Indeed, teachers often mirror this belief system and create classroom environments that are based on this individualistic way of being. Conversely, many cultures represent a collectivistic view in which group harmony or the good of the group is more important than are individual rights, and a person's value is judged by his or her sacrifice of individualism in favor of a group (DeCapua & Marshal, 2010; Hofstede, 2001; Hofstede & Hofstede, 2005; Zacarian & Haynes, 2012). Collectivism is reflected in the cultures of many students whose family origins are Latin, Central, and South America as well as Asia, the Middle East, and Africa (Haynes, 2008; Hofstede, 2001; Hofstede & Hofstede, 2005). The importance of culture cannot be overstated. While some of us may favor an alternative to paired and group work because of our strong belief in individualism, it may be an exclusionary method that is not reflective of all of our students' ways of being and acting. A collaborative paired and group work approach is more likely to be valued by students from collectivist cultures because it is so connected to a core cultural belief. As such, it is a prime space for many students to apprentice academic language, and the effort is well worth it.

The following reflection prompts have been separated for individual study and team study. Complete the prompt that applies to your particular context.

REFLECTION PROMPT FOR INDIVIDUAL STUDY

Time for Reflection:

Reflect on the following question, and write a response.

- Identify your own orientation (individualist or collectivist), and discuss how it is or is not in sync with your students and the steps that you might need to take to expand your knowledge about different orientations in your work.

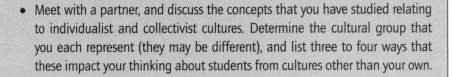

REFLECTION PROMPT FOR TEAM STUDY AND OUR-O-LOGUE

Time for Reflection:

Reflect on the following question, write a response, and prepare to discuss it with your team.

- Meet with a partner, and discuss the concepts that you have studied relating to individualist and collectivist cultures. Determine the cultural group that you each represent (they may be different), and list three to four ways that these impact your thinking about students from cultures other than your own.

PROCESS AND TASKS ELEMENTS OF GROUP WORK

Paired and group work has many implied rules that must be explicitly taught to students. Consider the classroom in which the teacher says, "Talk to the person next to you about this question, and we will then talk about it as a whole class." This simple directive has many hidden expectations. First, that the pair of students will know to participate actively with each other in the process of paired work and will complete the assigned task successfully. These two elements, process and task, are distinct and essential elements of group work (Bailey, 1996; Cohen, 1994, 1998; Cohen & Lotan, 1995, 1997; Zacarian, 2011b). The process component has to do with students engaging actively in the interactive activity of working together.

Whether it is in a pair or a group, the social activity of engaging as a collective will not necessarily happen on its own, even when students know the rules for participating. Why? Group work is an entirely complex endeavor that is filled with implied understandings about status and positional power from an individualistic and group standpoint. Take, for example, a group of students in a general science classroom. Some may come from what Cohen (1994, 1998) and Cohen and Lotan (1995, 1997) aptly describe as positions of high status, and others from positions of low status. The ones with the most perceived status (based on either their own perception or the perception of others) are more likely to participate, whereas students with the least are less likely to do so. These perceptions may come from personal or collective beliefs about socioeconomic or popularity status and other factors, and they affect who is active in the process. Because group work and learning require an active process, we have to consider ways to make it active for everyone and remedy the status elements.

Not surprisingly, students and their groups need help to engage in group work successfully and to understand the implied and explicit tasks and processes. Chiu (2004) describes this as *teacher interventions* and states that they should be used when problems occur. For example, a teacher might note that a group is moving off-task or does not seem to be working well together. In a review of the research on this topic, Chiu found that it is helpful when teachers provide a brief intervention and then allow the group to continue to work together. Interventions of this nature help the process of group work markedly. However, Chiu also notes that students were less likely to ask for help when it was needed. Perhaps this is a face-saving measure or the politics of status at work. Regardless, group work requires a high level of monitoring each group's process.

Various activities have been found to be helpful in the process elements (Cohen & Lotan, 1995, 1997; Haynes & Zacarian, 2010; Zacarian, 2011b;

Zacarian & Haynes, 2012). Of particular note are the means by which teachers assign status to all of their students in ways that are real and honoring as well as essential to the group's work. Let's revisit Mrs. Delgado's biology class to examine this more closely. In her class are a variety of ninth-grade students. Some are from high-status and others low-status experiences. One in particular, Michael, rarely speaks in class. Mrs. Delgado knows that he has had several failing grades in other subjects and that he often views himself as one of the "dumbest kids in the school" (his words). When Mrs. Delgado shows the movie *Life's Greatest Miracle* to her class, she genuinely wants Michael participate in the group activity. To do this, she first divides the class into pairs and then places them into small cooperative learning groups of four students each. She assigns one student from each group to make note of who speaks and the type of contribution that they make. She defines the different types of contributions that each participant might make and asks for suggestions. "You might discuss what you see on this poster. What else might be included," she asks, "in our list of what we think we might see?" Figure 3.2 provides the four most common categories that the whole class suggested. Mrs. Delgado asks a member from each group to note the types of examples that are provided. Figure 3.2 also provides her with a tally sheet of who participated and who didn't, and it is a helpful means for Mrs. Delgado to see who needs to be contributing more or less.

Figure 3.2   Contribution Tally Sheet

	Suggesting a passage from the course text	Pointing to a picture in the course text	Drawing from a personal example	Suggesting an example from displays in the classroom
Michael		///		/
Tonya	///// //			//
James	/////	////		/
Charlene		///// /////		/////

Source: Adapted from Zacarian (2011b).

The following reflection prompts have been separated for individual study and team study. Complete the prompt that applies to your particular context.

REFLECTION PROMPT FOR INDIVIDUAL STUDY

Time for Reflection:

Reflect on the following questions, and write responses.

- In what ways do you think that tallying the contributions of each student might support active participation?

- What additional strategies might you use to support the process element of group work?

REFLECTION PROMPT FOR TEAM STUDY AND OUR-O-LOGUE

Time for Reflection:

Reflect on the following questions, write responses, and prepare to discuss them with your team.

- Plan to observe a classroom setting, perhaps your own, in which a group of students will be engaged in collaborative work. Use your knowledge of the topic and Figure 3.2 to create a tally sheet that will document the

(Continued)

(Continued)

number and types of communication that each student will engage in. Observe the group in action. Use the tally sheet to note who speaks, and document your findings here.

• Drawing from the completed tally sheet, discuss your observations in terms of what you noted and what you might do to elicit a lower or higher level of interaction among the students who spoke too little, too much, and so on.

While the process task is occurring, Mrs. Delgado asks another member of the group to note the five most common things that the group expects to see in the movie. Each group spends a fair amount of time on this task. When it is completed, Mrs. Delgado asks each group to report the most common things that they believe they will see. She lists these on the board and then furnishes each student with a sticker. She asks students to place a sticker next to the thing that they believe they will see. These activities are reflective of the task element of group work. To do this well, we must create activities that are compelling so that students will want to do them and are invested in the learning process. Creating compelling tasks has to be reflective of the first element of this sociocultural frame—learning must build connections to what is socially relevant and personal to students' lives. When this occurs, students will be far more likely to actively participate in learning. Creating tasks and activities that are compelling must take into account the various literacy levels of students, the academic tasks, and students' thinking skills.

PUTTING THE SOCIOCULTURAL FRAME INTO PRACTICE

Build strong relationships with students

- Empathetically understand each student.
- Know students' interests.
- Personally connect with each student.
- Infuse this understanding into the learning environment.
- Help students see value in learning and their future.

Connect curriculum with students' lives to create a context-rich learning environment

- Ground learning in students' personal, cultural, language, and world experiences.
- Connect curriculum to issues that are socially relevant to students (including social justice issues).
- Help students take a critical stance on socially relevant issues through these curriculum connections.

Engage students in paired and small-group work

- Consistently use flexible grouping strategies.
- Model expectations of pair and group process and tasks.
- Assign students pair and group roles as appropriate (e.g., listener, speaker, note-taker), and rotate these roles so that students can enact each of them.
- Provide opportunities for students to give feedback about the process and product of pair and group work.

SUMMARY

In this chapter, we discussed the importance of the sociocultural frame. We described how the content to be learned must be connected to students' personal, cultural, and world knowledge. We also discussed the importance of connecting curriculum to issues that are socially relevant to students. We provided three classroom examples of how this works in the planning and delivery of curriculum. We also discussed the importance of understanding culture from collectivist and individualist perspectives and creating classroom configurations that match the cultural orientations of our students. In addition, we discussed learning as an interactive process that gives students multiple practice opportunities to apprentice in academic language interactions. To do this effectively, we must use explicit instructions in the process and task elements of group work. We also looked at suggestions for putting these ideas into practice.

In Chapter 4, we will look more closely at the second area of the four-pronged framework: learning as a developmental process.

REFERENCES

Bailey, F. (1996). The role of collaborative dialogue in teacher education. In D. Freeman & J. C. Richards (Eds.), *Teacher learning in language teaching* (pp. 260–280). New York, NY: Cambridge University Press.

Balfanz, R., & Byrnes, V. (2012). *Chronic absenteeism: Summarizing what we know from nationally available data.* Baltimore, MD: Johns Hopkins University, Center for Social Organization of Schools.

Chiu, M. M. (2004). Adapting teacher interventions to student needs during cooperative learning: How to improve student problem solving and time on task. *American Educational Research Journal, 41,* 365–399.

Cohen, E. G. (1994). *Designing groupwork: Strategies for heterogeneous classrooms* (2nd ed.). New York, NY: Teachers College Press.

Cohen, E. G. (1998). Making cooperative learning equitable. *Educational Leadership, 56,* 18–21.

Cohen, E. G., & Lotan, R. A. (1995). Producing equal-status interaction in heterogeneous classrooms. *American Education Research Journal, 32,* 99–120.

Cohen, E. G., & Lotan, R. A. (Eds.). (1997). *Working for equity in heterogeneous classrooms: Sociological theory in practice.* New York, NY: Teachers College Press.

DeCapua, A., & Marshal, H. (2010). Serving ELLs with limited or interrupted education: Intervention that works. *TESOL Journal, 1,* 49–70. Retrieved from http://www.tesolmedia.com/docs/TJ/firstissue/06_TJ_DeCapuaMarshall.pdf

Freire, P. (1970). *Pedagogy of the oppressed.* New York, NY: Herder & Herder.

Haynes, J. (2008). *Getting started with English language learners: How educators can meet the challenge.* Alexandria, VA: Association for Supervision and Curriculum Development.

Haynes, J., & Zacarian, D. (2010). *Teaching English language learners across the content areas.* Alexandria, VA: Association for Supervision and Curriculum Development.

Hofstede, G. (2001). *Cultures consequences: Comparing values, behaviors, institutions, and organizations across nations* (2nd ed.). Thousand Oaks, CA: Sage

Hofstede, G., & Hofstede, G. J. (2005). *Cultures and organizations: Software of the mind* (2nd ed.). New York, NY: McGraw-Hill.

Massachusetts Department of Education. (2006). *Massachusetts science and technology/engineering curriculum framework.* Retrieved from http://www.doe.mass.edu/frameworks/scitech/1006.pdf

Vasquez, V. (2010). Critical literacy isn't just for books anymore. *The Reading Teacher, 63,* 614–616.

WGBH Educational Foundation. (1996–2012). *Life's greatest miracle.* Retrieved from http://www.pbs.org/wgbh/nova/body/life-greatest-miracle.html

Zacarian, D. (2011a). Making data-driven decisions based on effective measures of English learner performance: How ESAs can provide support. *Perspectives, 17,* 61–66.

Zacarian, D. (2011b). *Transforming schools for English learners: A comprehensive guide for school leaders.* Thousand Oaks, CA: Corwin.

Zacarian, D., & Haynes, J. (2012). *The essential guide to educating English learners.* Thousand Oaks, CA: Corwin.

Zacarian, D. (1996). *Learning how to teach and design curriculum for the heterogeneous class: An ethnographic study of a task-based cooperative learning group of native English and English as a second language speakers in a graduate education course* (Master's thesis). Available from ProQuest Dissertations and Theses database. (UMI No. 9639055)

Zwiers, J., & Crawford, M. (2011). *Academic conversations: Classroom talk that fosters critical thinking and content understandings.* Portland, ME: Stenhouse.

4 Learning as a Developmental Process

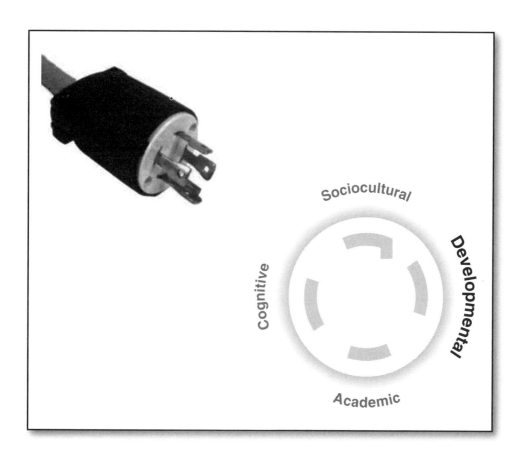

Why is it important to explicitly teach and mentor students in academic language and literacy behaviors?

We begin our discussion of the second prong of our four-pronged framework by visiting Mrs. Shumway's English class and meeting Eric, one of her students.

Eric is a student in Mrs. Shumway's eighth-grade English class. Mrs. Shumway is teaming with one of the eighth-grade social studies teachers, Mr. Cantor, to conduct an interdisciplinary unit of study on the Civil War. Mrs. Shumway and Mr. Cantor believe strongly that their students learn best with and from each other. They frequently engage students in activities that require a high level of participation.

For the English language arts culminating activity of this unit, Mrs. Shumway separates her class into four cooperative learning groups. She says, "Each group will represent a family that is from either the North or the South and has members who are fighting in the war." She assigns two groups to be from the South and two from the North and says, "Your group will engage in writing letters between family members who are fighting in the war and members who remain at home. Groups will assign a role to each member of their team, such as a father and son who are fighting in the war and a mother and sister who remain at home. You will also decide on the setting in which the letter writing will take place and base it on what you will be studying."

In the English language arts and social studies classes, the students will see movies about the Civil War, listen to guest speakers discuss the Civil War, read the novel *The Red Badge of Courage* (Crane, 1895), and read a chapter on the Civil War in their social studies text.

"The letters that you will write," Mrs. Shumway tells them, "will be read aloud by each group and will depict the emotions and realities of each family member. What must it have been like to have a family member fight in the war? What might a husband write to his wife about it or a brother to his sister? We will think carefully about this in our groups to make it as real as possible." Mrs. Shumway also tells them that this letter-writing activity will represent 15% of their final grade.

Eric is concerned about this participation. He loves Mrs. Shumway and the class but worries that his writing skills are not strong enough for him to do well in the letter-writing task. He tries hard to cover his insecurities with a level of bravado intended to keep his classmates and Mrs. Shumway from knowing his difficulties with writing. While reading the novel and social studies text will be particularly challenging, he is quite capable of listening carefully in class and looking as if he can participate actively in class discussions. For example, in pair and group work, he extends the dialogue by referencing what his peers say and extending their discussion. The writing task is a different story.

Let's look closely at what we mean by literacy behaviors and their relationship with academic achievement. To do this, we'll revisit the concepts of students who carry academic language versus those who are learning academic language. Students who carry academic language generally grow up in homes and communities where literacy is present. These include students from rural, suburban, and urban environments and students who represent a range of socioeconomic experiences. What is common among students who carry academic language is that they listen, speak, read, and write a variation of English that matches the language that is used in school and what is often referred to as *school language* (Soto-Hinman & Hetzel, 2009; Zwiers, 2007a, 2007b) and what Delpit (1995) refers to as *middle-class speech.*

THE LITERACY SUITCASE

Chapter 2 described the literacy behaviors of learners who carry academic language. They can be symbolized as the contents of a suitcase that students carry into and out of school. The literacy suitcase, in a figurative sense, is packed with rich vocabulary; literacy as a cultural way of being and acting; an understanding of how to complete activities requiring organizational, problem-solving, and decision-making skills that match what is done in school; what it means to be a learner; the ability to generalize from the specific; and dialect skills that are similar to language used in classrooms. Learners who own these behaviors are distinct from students who are just learning them. The former possess certain skills that the latter do not. Gaining these skills requires additional work by academic language learners that can occur only when their teachers create space for this essential learning to occur. In this chapter, we will focus on four of the contents of the literacy suitcase: literacy as a developmental process, literacy as cultural way of being and acting, understanding literacy as a functional process, and building rich vocabulary. To begin this discussion, let's look more closely at what it means to be an academic language learner.

LITERACY AS A DEVELOPMENTAL PROCESS

Academic language learners represent groups that are reared in communities and homes that use wide variations of English and other languages, including, but not limited to, African American English, Chicano English, and

English represented among different indigenous American communities in places such as Alaska, Hawaii, and elsewhere (Labov, 2006; Soto-Hinman & Hetzel, 2009). While many hear and carry academic language, academic language learners speak a dialect that does not match the type of academic language that is needed in school.

Academic language learners need what Soto-Hinman and Hetzel (2009) refer to as *linguistic mentorships*. They draw from many of the same theories and best practices that occur for English learners in three key ways. First, students' language usage (regardless of dialect) is acknowledged and valued. Second, there is an intentional effort to contrast students' home language with school language so that they are exposed regularly to the differences and are mentored to preserve both while at the same time begin carrying the literacy suitcase regularly. Finally, students are fully supported, mentored, and empowered to succeed in school using the same literacy suitcase as their peers.

Academic language learning communities use language that is rich and well developed and marks the unique culture in which they live. However, a primary difference is that it does not match what is needed to be successful, and is used, in school. In addition, academic language learners are less likely to have an abundance of continuous routine out-of-school experiences hearing and using school language. While they come to school with rich language systems, it is in a language that does not match what is occurring in school and results, more often than not, in a clear divide between those who carry academic language and are successful in school and those who do not. This literacy gap, as referred to by Soto-Hinman and Hetzel (2009), has resulted in an ever-present reminder of the failures of our schools to successfully address the needs of this large and growing group of students. Indeed, they refer to the gap as a state of emergency for learners who do not possess or carry the language of school.

Soto-Hinman and Hetzel (2009) argue that there is an urgent need for educators to draw from the findings of the National Literacy Panel (August & Shanahan, 2006) as a core means for closing the literacy gap. The National Literacy Panel consisted of a "group of experts-researchers in reading, language, bilingualism, research methods, and education" (p. x) who were charged with the following:

> to identify, assess, and synthesize research on the education of language minority children and youth with respect to their attainment of literacy, and to produce a comprehensive report evaluating and synthesizing this literature. (p. 1)

Let's look more closely at the developmental elements of literacy, as discussed by the National Literacy Panel.

Development of Literacy: The Role of Listening, Speaking, and Experiencing

Literacy learning is a developmental process that is dependent on a variety of elements including a student's age, prior learning experiences, and proficiency in oral language. Indeed, spoken language (i.e., what a child hears and uses from birth) plays an essential role in the development of literacy and school readiness, as we shall see. What we hear and how we use language are important features of how we prepare for school. Students who have well-developed vocabulary, listening, and speaking skills are far more likely to be successful than are students who do not possess these much-needed school language skills. Think of students who come from countries from across the globe, such as Nigeria, Japan, or Puerto Rico. If these students possess well-developed vocabulary, listening, and speaking skills and higher-order thinking skills in their native language, it is highly likely that they will transfer these skills into English (Lesaux, Koda, Seigel, & Shanahan, 2006). However, the same cannot be said for students who come from the same countries but do not possess these core skills, and this holds true as well for many students who are U.S.-born and monolingual English speaking.

Many of these early developmental literacy skills are not as obviously connected to what one might think of as literacy per se, as no print is involved. Consider the 3-year-old who is visiting a local aquarium with her parents. They are viewing an exhibit that includes small and large fish. "Which fish do you think might eat the most food? The big or the little fish?" the mother asks. When her child responds, she asks another question, "Why do you think that the big fish eats more than the little fish?" This question-and-answer sequence requires many processing skills of the 3-year-old and requires a high level of executive function. She must draw from her background knowledge, infer, simultaneously understand the structure and meaning of what is being asked, and respond accordingly, among other things.

Literacy is a process that begins at early ages, long before a child begins to read. Lesaux et al. (2006) examined the relationships between listening and speaking, children's awareness of print, and reading ability. They found a strong relationship between understanding of oral language and ability to draw from these skills to develop reading and writing skills. Indeed, their analysis reveals that the students with the oral ability to rapidly name numbers, letters, and objects had fewer reading challenges than did students who could not perform these tasks as well.

When we think of reading, we have to think of it as a development process. Pransky (2008, p. 115) describes the reading process as beginning with our first seeing a "squiggle" and then "squiggles" on a page that our brain processes into letters, words, contexts, and meaning. Look at Figure 4.1, and see if you can read what it says.

For those of us who read Arabic, we might know that these squiggles form separate letters and the letters form the word for *hello*. For those of us who have not had sufficient exposure to the Arabic symbol system, they remain what Pransky calls squiggles on a page. Continuous exposure is an important feature here. Hinkel (2009) likens it to a person—let's call him John—who moves to a new city and starts a new job. John will have to work to find his new workplace the first time. He might get lost along the way without a map, GPS, or other source of support. During the second trip to work, John might recognize some of the buildings and signs that mark his way to work. He might remember even more the next time. This *learn where the place is* activity takes many times before it all becomes routine enough so that it can be done automatically. In the same sense, making squiggles into letters, letters into sounds, sounds into words, words into sentences, sentences into paragraphs, and so forth does not become automatic without a large amount of exposure and use—much more than John needed to get comfortable finding his way to work. It is through continuous and repeated exposure and use that literacy practices become automatic.

Recently, I saw a bumper sticker that stated, "If you can read this, thank a teacher!" Now, while I do think that teachers do many great

Figure 4.1

Source: Thanks to Shaimaa H. Moustafa of the University of Massachusetts Arabic Language Department.

things, reading does not generally occur in a vacuum in a classroom. It occurs through the repetition of events that occur over and over and over again that leads to one becoming a reader. For some of our students, it is a reflection of their family and community's way of being and acting.

LITERACY AS A CULTURAL WAY OF BEING AND ACTING

Our contexts and home communities play an important role in making sense of the print that we see (Eggins, 2005; Gee, 1990; Pransky, 2008). We use our personal, world, cultural, linguistic, and academic knowledge to process information at multiple levels, including sentence, paragraph, section, chapter, and so forth. These acts involve much higher levels of processing and linguistic demands (Lesaux et al., 2006; Pransky, 2008). We move from reading squiggles to making meaning of what we read to making predictions, inferences, and more, and we build these understandings from our knowledge of the world around us. While the acts of inferencing and predicting will be discussed in much more detail in Chapter 6, when we look more closely at learning as a cognitive process, we must think of literacy as being situated in a sociocultural context that is dependent on our personal, world, cultural, and linguistic experience. In a real sense, it is the coming together of these experiences and the knowledge that we gain from them that forms what we know of as literacy. The research points to the reality that knowledge of word meaning and repeated exposure to understanding and using words are critical to success in reading.

Let's return to Mrs. Shumway's class and look at her assignment to understand how this works in practice. For Eric to complete the letter-writing project, he has to have knowledge about how the English language works so that he can read information at the word, sentence, paragraph, and chapter levels; the Civil War; family relationships; different settings where families lived and the war was fought; and the proper form for letter writing. This requires that he have broad vocabulary and comprehension skills in a range of areas and that he multitask all of these elements at once to complete the letter-writing task that he has been assigned. The National Literacy Panel found vocabulary and comprehension to be key challenges for many students (Lesaux et al., 2006). These skills are items that must be included in a literacy suitcase. They are key requirements for a person who carries academic language.

To understand concepts, according to Fang and Schleppegrell (2008), Eggins (2005), and Pransky (2008), we have to understand that part of the reading process must also include an understanding of what the author intends for us to read. That is, we must understand that language is functional. We use language to make meaning, and we make meaning through our understanding of the sociocultural context (Fang & Schleppegrell, 2010; Halliday, 1994). Take, for example, a retelling of the Civil War. Readers would need to understand the time period, living conditions, reasons for the war, and much more to understand the true meaning of the retelling.

Of course a retelling is one type of writing. There are many others. Let's look at three sections as they appear in the very beginning of the chapter that Eric will read in his social studies textbook. They represent the same sequence that opens each chapter of his textbook and takes up only a fraction of the actual chapter:

> **American Diary:** At the Battle of Malvern Hill in 1862, a Union sergeant named Driscoll shot a young Confederate soldier. Hurrying forward, Driscoll turned the soldier's face up to see if the young man was dead. But when he looked at the dying soldier's face, he received a terrible shock. Looking up, the boy murmured, "Father" and then closed his eyes forever. The soldier was his son who had gone south before the war.
>
> **Main Idea:** The North and South had many different strengths, strategies, and purposes in the Civil War.
>
> **History and You:** Is it better for an army to have plenty of soldiers or the powerful will to fight? Why? Read and learn how these characteristics affected the Civil War. (Appleby, Brinkley, Broussard, McPherson, & Ritchie, 2009, pp. 474–475)

UNDERSTANDING LITERACY AS A FUNCTIONAL PROCESS

An understanding of subject matter comes from the ways in which text is written. What does this mean? Fang and Schleppegrell (2010), Freeman and Freeman (2009), and Halliday (1994, 2003) offer important insights for us to consider in terms of how to help students understand how subject-specific text is written. An important means for doing this is to help students learn how language is used, especially in subject-specific texts, how this relates to its meaning, how its meaning is influenced by the context in which it is written, and how the context is influenced by a specific genre or medium.

Take, for example, a story. According to Fang and Schleppegrell, children's books generally use nontechnical vocabulary and simple clauses.

Importantly, they generally resemble the type of oral speech that is somewhat familiar to most students. Consider the following excerpt from *Harry Potter and the Sorcerer's Stone* (Rowling, 1997):

Example 1

The storm raged more and more ferociously as the night went on. Harry couldn't sleep. He shivered and turned over, trying to get comfortable, his stomach rumbling with hunger. Dudley's snores were drowned by the low rolls of thunder that started near midnight. The lighted dial of Dudley's watch, which was dangling over the edge of the sofa on his fat wrist, told Harry that he'd be eleven in ten minutes' time. He lay and watched his birthday tick nearer, wondering if the Dursleys would remember at all, wondering where the letter writer was now. (p. 45)

The language from this example is not technical or dependent on specific-subject matter. It is also fluid and written in a format or language pattern that is familiar to many students who are familiar with storytelling. Further, while it includes many descriptive words, such as *raged* and *ferociously*, it does not veer too far from the patterns that are used in everyday communication. Subject-specific genre is distinct from storytelling narrative and what we use in everyday speech. Let's look at Eric's social studies text as an example.

Example 2

For most states, choosing sides in the Civil War was easy. The border states of Delaware, Maryland, Kentucky, and Missouri, however, were bitterly divided. Slavery was legal in all four states, though none had many enslaved people. All four had ties to the North and the South.

These states were vital to the Union because of their strategic locations. Missouri could control parts of the Mississippi River and major routes to the west. Kentucky controlled the Ohio River. Delaware was close to Philadelphia. (Appleby et al., 2009, p. 475)

This text deals with a specific topic, the Civil War, and uses language patterns that are unlike the patterns found in the story. Where Example 1 contains language that is typically found in daily speech, Example 2 contains language that is specific to the subject (*choosing sides, border states, and enslaved people*) and needs to be learned. Also, it uses long phrases

(*The border states of Delaware, Maryland, Kentucky, and Missouri*). In general, subject matter text, such as that in Example 2, veers sharply away from the type of text that students, especially academic language learners, are familiar with. Why? It contains a good deal of technical or subject-specific language that can make it particularly challenging to understand.

The following reflection prompts have been separated for individual study and team study. Complete the prompt that applies to your particular context.

REFLECTION PROMPT FOR INDIVIDUAL STUDY

Time for Reflection:

Reflect on the following question, and write a response.

Read the following excerpt from a biology textbook.

Example 3

Where do you think most of the world's photosynthesis takes place? You may think it occurs in tropical rain forests. Or maybe you think it occurs in the vast evergreen forest in northern regions. These would be good guesses, but they are not correct. Most photosynthesis occurs in the oceans.

The upper layers of the oceans are home to microscopic organisms called plankton. Some plankton, such as bacteria and algae, carry out photosynthesis. These plankton are called phytoplankton. Although tiny, phytoplankton are very important. (Park & Enderle, 2006, p. 241)

- While the text includes short sentences and a few embedded clauses, what do you think makes it more difficult to understand than the *Harry Potter* text found in Example 1?

**REFLECTION PROMPT FOR TEAM
STUDY AND OUR-O-LOGUE**

Time for Reflection:

Reflect on the following questions, write responses, and prepare to discuss them with your team.
Read the following excerpt from a biology textbook.

Example 3

Where do you think most of the world's photosynthesis takes place? You may think it occurs in tropical rain forests. Or maybe you think it occurs in the vast evergreen forest in northern regions. These would be good guesses, but they are not correct. Most photosynthesis occurs in the oceans.

The upper layers of the oceans are home to microscopic organisms called plankton. Some plankton, such as bacteria and algae, carry out photosynthesis. These plankton are called phytoplankton. Although tiny, phytoplankton are very important. (Park & Enderle, 2006, p. 241)

- With a partner, discuss the following: While the text includes short sentences and a few embedded clauses, what do you think makes it more difficult to understand than the *Harry Potter* text found in Example 1?

- With a partner, select a passage from a course textbook and a book written for pleasure reading for the same grade level. Discuss the reasons why you think the course text is more difficult to understand than the book written for pleasure. How are the reasons similar to the first task that you completed?

Example 3, found in the individual and collaborative reflection tasks, includes a good deal of challenging text and what Fang and Schleppegrell (2010) refer to as *a heavy load* of technical vocabulary. In addition, it is filled with language that is connected by linking verbs that are common in science (e.g., *are called*). For students to understand science text, they have to understand the way it is expressed. Mathematics is also written in a language-patterned way.

The following reflection prompts have been separated for individual study and team study. Complete the prompt that applies to your particular context.

REFLECTION PROMPT FOR INDIVIDUAL STUDY

Time for Reflection:

Reflect on the following questions, and write responses.
Read each of the following math problems, and reflect on what you read that is familiar to you about how mathematics problems are presented.

- Mary went flower picking. She picked 8 flowers. Each flower has 10 petals. How many petals are there altogether?

- Matt bought 16 tickets at the amusement park. If the Tilt-a-Whirl ride costs 6 tickets, the Ferris Wheel costs 10 tickets, the Swing-a-Round costs 4 tickets, and the Water Slide costs 4 tickets, what is the maximum number of rides that Matt can take?

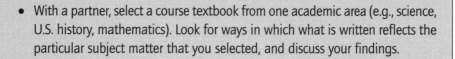

REFLECTION PROMPT FOR TEAM STUDY AND OUR-O-LOGUE

Time for Reflection:

Reflect on the following question, write a response, and prepare to discuss it with your team.

- With a partner, select a course textbook from one academic area (e.g., science, U.S. history, mathematics). Look for ways in which what is written reflects the particular subject matter that you selected, and discuss your findings.

Each discipline has its own distinct language and way of communicating. Consider carpentry, plumbing, graphic arts, and machine shop classes in a vocational setting. The language of each shop is quite specific; we can expect that its teachers will be using this specific language when they teach and that the texts included in these shops will as well. Who is the best teacher to teach the language of content? Subject matter teachers. However, we don't all consider ourselves to be language teachers (Freeman & Freeman, 2009), and we should! One way of doing this is to understand that the language of content is written in a particular way and that an important part of our work is to help students understand the specific type of language expression that is used. This type of understanding is referred to as *systemic functional linguistics* (Fang & Schleppegrell, 2010; Halliday, 1994). Rather than teaching facts and information (e.g., what plankton is, how to solve a math problem), we must teach how the language of the subject matter is expressed.

BUILDING RICH VOCABULARY

While all students need phonological abilities to read words (Lesaux et al., 2006), key influencers of reading include a student's vocabulary knowledge (Lesaux et al., 2006; Nation, 2001), prior experience with print and literacy (Lesaux et al., 2006), and an understanding of the context in which it is used. It requires that Eric have some knowledge about how the textbook is written. For example, he would have to know that the section labeled American Diary involves a certain type of recording that is not personal, as most diaries are. For him to understand the section labeled Main Idea, he would have to have an understanding of three concepts (*strengths, strategies,* and *purposes*) as being distinct and would have to know how to apply these to the key concepts that he is studying. In addition, he would have to know what some of the key phrases mean so that he can understand them in context. This includes the idiomatic expression embedded in the sentence: "his son who had *gone south* before the war." Thus vocabulary concepts, including terms, words, idioms, and phrases— what I refer to as TWIPs—are key to his understanding of the content.

Whether a learner is a monolingual speaker of American English or an English learner, vocabulary is always situated in a sociocultural context and greatly influences comprehension in two important ways: Students need a rich and well-developed vocabulary to do well in school, and they have to be able to use the vocabulary at will. Take, for example, the word *couch* as a noun. What is another word that you might use as a substitute? You might use *sofa, divan, love seat,* and so forth. Now, if *couch* is used as a verb, it has an entirely different meaning, including to express, phrase, or formulate. A simple word such as *couch* used as a verb in a sentence drastically changes the meaning from what it would be if used as a noun. For example, let's look at a hypothetical sentence that might have been written in the American Diary section of Eric's course text:

> When Driscoll wrote his wife about their son's death, he *couched* his retelling sensitively so that his wife would not think that he was a monster.

Fang and Schleppegrell (2010) and Pransky (2008) claim that understanding an author's meaning is critical for students. Pransky has found that some students cannot see themselves as separate from what they are reading. Their world view may be somewhat limited by the constraints of their own lives. He has found that many students who have difficulties learning new concepts are challenged in trying to comprehend the author's full meaning. In the example from the course text, Eric would have to understand that the son not only moved away from his family but went to live and fight in a new community that was the enemy of his father's. In this case, the authors might have been trying to personalize the war experience and show how families were torn apart. For Eric to understand this concept, he would have to know that the authors' language and meaning are entirely different from Eric's context and experience, and that he might be challenged to understand the text with the same meaning as do his peers who have an understanding about what authors are trying to do and convey.

The following reflection prompts have been separated for individual study and team study. Complete the prompt that applies to your particular context.

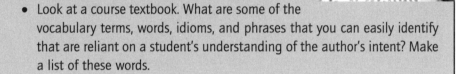

REFLECTION PROMPT FOR INDIVIDUAL STUDY

Time for Reflection:

Reflect on the following question, and write a response.

- Look at a course textbook. What are some of the vocabulary terms, words, idioms, and phrases that you can easily identify that are reliant on a student's understanding of the author's intent? Make a list of these words.

REFLECTION PROMPT FOR TEAM STUDY AND OUR-O-LOGUE

Time for Reflection:

Reflect on the following questions, write responses, and prepare to discuss them with your team.

- With a partner, look at a course text that includes a good volume of written language. Come to agreement about the key terms, words, idioms, and phrases that you believe are reliant on students' understanding of what the author intended.

(Continued)

(Continued)

- What strategies would you use for teaching these to students?

Building rich vocabulary requires an understanding of key elements. First, that language is always used in context and each context is driven by its special purpose. Accordingly, TWIPs, or what we call vocabulary, are always nested in a context. The example used earlier about *couch* as a noun and a verb is a fine example of how language is used in context. Second, vocabulary instruction, that is, the teaching of TWIPs, must take place in an environment that is context rich, be intentional, comprise multiple and consistent practice opportunities to use them in context, and include ways to help students learn new vocabulary on their own (Blachowicz & Fisher, 2002; Webb, 2007). In my work with teachers, I often see word walls that do not have context cues. In some classes, words are organized alphabetically, and in others the word walls contain lists of words that appear in a course text. This type of vocabulary instruction, though perhaps intentional, is not intentional in a way that matches the vocabulary learning needs of academic language learners.

Noted psychologist Howard Gardner (2009) describes how important is it for us to consider what is really needed by our students when we teach them. What do academic language learners need to learn vocabulary? Intentionality! Random lists of words, whether written alphabetically or in the sequence of a course text, are not intentional enough because they are not nested in a context that students can readily understand. A first and important concept in packing their literacy suitcase is knowing that words are learned in context and that we must take time to determine the key words that are needed for students to be able to learn the content and context. A second and equally important element is providing students with multiple exposures and practice opportunities, as many as ten or more, to learn new vocabulary (Webb, 2007).

Understanding Different Types of Vocabulary

Beck, McKeown, and Kucan (2002) describe three tiers of vocabulary:

1. Common, everyday words

2. More sophisticated, useful synonyms of Tier 1 words

3. Academic terms and sophisticated words that are generally not synonyms of Tier 1 words

Tier 1 words are the ones that we use to communicate simple everyday vocabulary. Words such as *like* and *eat* are Tier 1 words. *I like to eat breakfast* is a sentence that contains Tier 1 vocabulary to describe what I like to do in everyday life. Tier 1 words are generally one syllable, and we use them to describe the world around us.

Tier 2 words are synonyms of the basic Tier 1 vocabulary. They are generally more descriptive words that allow us to be more detailed and specific. For example, here is a sentence that uses the Tier 1 word *like: John likes Amy*. There are many more descriptive words for describing the degree of feelings that John has for Amy (e.g., *He finds her pleasant, He adores Amy*). What is critical for us to know is that academic language learners do not have a large repertoire of Tier 2 words, and they need them so that they can be more detailed, specific, and successful in school (Beck et al., 2002; Pransky, 2008; Zwiers, 2007a). Students who carry academic language not only know and use the word *like* but can also automatically switch to more detailed language when it is needed.

An example of the difference between students who carry academic language and academic language learners is an overuse of Tier 1 words among the latter group of students. It is common to see students use the same word over and over again because they do not have the repertoire that is needed in the rich vocabulary contents of their suitcase.

Tier 2 words need to be taught directly and explicitly. Academic researchers and scholars Hart and Risley (1995), Calderón, (2007), and Calderón and Minaye-Rowe (2011) help us understand the importance of directly teaching these words. A helpful tool for supporting Tier 2 development is to help students visually see synonyms for common Tier 1 words. This is especially true for words that are commonly overused. Another important strategy is to graphically display additional word choices to reflect degree and intensity. For example, *good* may be an overused Tier 1 word. Providing students with a visual of word choices that reflect the degree and intensity of the word, such *good, very good, great, terrific,* and *amazing,* can assist students in developing stronger and larger vocabularies.

Tier 3 words help us describe the world clearly and accurately. Tier 3 consists of academic vocabulary and instructional language that are likely to be taught in subject matter classrooms to all students. However, as we approach the various forms of Tier 3 words, we must think about the ones that are used generally across disciplines and the ones that are taught solely in context (Dutro & Moran, 2003).

Zwiers (2007a) separates vocabulary into what he refers to as brick-and-mortar words. He uses the word *brick* to describe words that are subject or discipline specific. The words *reflection* and *refraction,* for example, are Tier 3 words used in science. Within the brick family are a range of words, from very concrete to more abstract. People, places, and things that can be described would be on the concrete side of the spectrum, whereas words such as *communism, socialism,* and *decomposition* would be brick words that are more abstract. Subject matter is filled with many brick words (which will be discussed further in Chapter 5). Mortar words, however, are the glue that binds language together and can be described as Tier 2 words (Zwiers, 2007a).

These are the types of words that are routinely used in classrooms but require that students have them in their literacy suitcases. *Maintain, require, tend, dimension, reality, correspond, inevitable, represent, account,* and *reflect* are mortar words (Zwiers, 2007a, p. 22). These words are generally not used in everyday communication, but they are used frequently in a variety of classroom contexts and elsewhere.

Also included in this category of Tier 2 words are transitional or connecting words that are synonyms of Tier 1 words. These connectors in Tier 1 language include *and, but,* and *so.* There are many mortar words that hold ideas together and, according to Zwiers, are commonly untaught and need to be.[1] Exposing students to these words is different from teaching them. The latter calls for the urgent need to provide the type of repeated and meaningful exposure that Hinkel (2009) refers to. It requires direct and explicit activities that engage students in practicing vocabulary authentically. An important strategy for doing this is to create a visual of additional word choices and to make these readily available for students. Figure 4.2

Figure 4.2 Word Wall of Additional Choices for Transition Words *And, But,* and *So*

And	But	So
Also	However	Consequently
Plus	Except	Accordingly
In addition	On the other hand	Thus
Moreover	Nevertheless	As a result

illustrates one type of visual that might be used. When students see these words, they have many more word choices.

The following reflection prompts have been separated for individual study and team study. Complete the prompt that applies to your particular context.

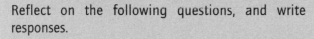

REFLECTION PROMPT FOR INDIVIDUAL STUDY

Time for Reflection:

Reflect on the following questions, and write responses.

- Look at text that you might use to teach. Identify some of the Tier 1, 2, and 3 words in it.

- Look at the same text, and identify the brick-and-mortar words.

**REFLECTION PROMPT FOR TEAM
STUDY AND OUR-O-LOGUE**

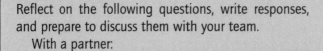

Time for Reflection:

Reflect on the following questions, write responses,
and prepare to discuss them with your team.
  With a partner:

- Look at text that you might use to teach. Come to agreement about some
  of the Tier 1, 2, and 3 words in it.

- Look at the same text, and identify the brick-and-mortar words.

- Look over the next section of this chapter, and create a word wall, table
  mat, or other device that will help students understand and use the words
  you have identified.

Word walls, table mats, handouts, and other devices are often used to display vocabulary words. Rather than including lists of what appear to be randomly selected words, separating words into categories such as people, places, and things is an important first step in teaching vocabulary. A second step is to connect vocabulary meaningfully to the content that is being studied. This meaningful context building is an essential means of helping academic language learners have a visual anchor. The word walls shown in Figures 4.3, 4.4, and 4.5 illustrate how this can occur.

Using these visual devices can greatly help students use the language of content in a more descriptive and intentional way. At the heart of academic literacy is this type of rich communication. That is, for students to carry academic language, they must be able to engage in "sustained and purposeful conversations about school topics" (Zwiers & Crawford, 2011, p. 1). The strategies and ideas that we have discussed are intended to support this goal.

Figure 4.3 Word Wall Used in an American History Lesson

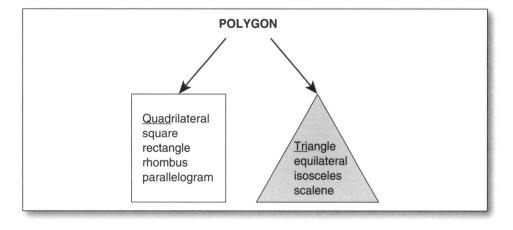

People	Places	Transportation	
Jane Addams	Tenement	Skyscraper	Elevator

Figure 4.4 Word Wall Used in a Mathematics Lesson

POLYGON

Quadrilateral
square
rectangle
rhombus
parallelogram

Triangle
equilateral
isosceles
scalene

Figure 4.5 Word Wall Used in an English Language Arts Lesson

Place	Money	What did Kalvin do with the coin?
Near a railroad track	Penny, nickel, dime, quarter	Flipped it
	Coins	Tossed it
		Used it to choose his cereal

PUTTING THE ACADEMIC LITERACY FRAME INTO PRACTICE

Understand literacy as a developmental process

- Understand literacy as a developmental process that is dependent on many elements, including a student's age, prior learning, and proficiency in oral language, as well as exposure to literacy practices.
- Mentor students to carry academic language through multiple purposeful practice opportunities that can support the automaticity of literacy practices.
- Use a high level of listening and speaking activities to support reading and writing.

Understand literacy as a cultural way of being and acting

- Understand, honor, and value the wide variations of English and other languages that students and families use.
- Know that students use their personal, world, cultural, linguistic, and academic language experiences to process information and make sense of it.

Understand literacy from a functional perspective

- Teach students how subject matter texts are written.
- Understand different types of vocabulary, and use sociocultural and academic context to teach it.
- Help students understand the writing and reading process.
- Support student understanding of author intent.
- Use visual devices to support vocabulary learning.
- Engage students in rich and purposeful academic conversations.

SUMMARY

This chapter discussed literacy as a learned behavior that encompasses what Soto-Hinman and Hetzel (2009) and Zwiers (2007a, 2007b) refer to as school language and Delpit (1985) as middle-class speech. We also discussed literacy as a developmental processes in which listening, speaking, and experiencing play essential roles. We drew from Hinkel (2009) to understand the need for multiple practice opportunities to move from learning language to using it automatically. We highlighted the essential need to teach students how subject matter texts are written, and we drew from Fang and Schleppegrell (2010) and Freeman and Freeman (2009) to explain these critical concepts. Finally, we discussed the importance of teaching vocabulary by engaging students in rich, text-specific academic conversations using the language of content, and drawing from, among others, Beck and colleagues' (2002) research on three tiers of vocabulary and Zwiers and Crawford's (2011) research on rich and purposeful academic interactions.

The next chapter will discuss the third prong of the four-pronged framework: learning as an academic process.

REFERENCES

Appleby, J., Brinkley, A., Broussard, A. S., McPherson, J. M., & Ritchie, D. A. (2009). *The American journey.* Columbus, OH: Glencoe/McGraw-Hill.

August, D., & Shanahan, T. (Eds.). (2006). *Developing literacy in second-language learners: A report of the National Literacy Panel on Language Minority Children and Youth.* Mahwah, NJ: Lawrence Erlbaum.

Beck, I., McKeown, M. G., & Kucan, L. (2002). *Bringing words to life: Robust vocabulary instruction.* New York, NY: Guilford Press.

Blachowicz, C., & Fisher, P. (2002). *Teaching vocabulary in all classrooms* (2nd ed.). Upper Saddle River, NJ: Pearson.

Calderón, M. (2007). *Teaching reading to English language learners, grades 6–12: A framework for improving achievement in the content areas.* Thousand Oaks, CA: Corwin.

Calderón, M. E., & Minaya-Rowe, L. (2011). *Preventing long-term ELs: Transforming schools to meet core standards.* Thousand Oaks, CA: Corwin.

Crane, S. (1895). *Red badge of courage.* New York, NY: D. Appleton.

Delpit, L. (1995). *Other people's children: Cultural conflict in the classroom.* New York, NY: New Press.

Eggins, S. (2005). *Introduction to systemic functional linguistics* (2nd ed.). New York, NY: Continuum.

Fang, Z., & Schleppegrell, M. J. (2010). Disciplinary literacies across content areas: Supporting reading through functional language analysis. *Journal of Adolescent & Adult Literacy, 53,* 587–597.

Freeman, Y. S., & Freeman, D. E. (2009). *Academic language for English language learners and struggling readers: How to help students succeed across content areas.* Portsmouth, NH: Heinemann.

Gardner, H. (2009). *Five minds for the future.* Watertown, MA: Harvard Business School.

Gee, J. P. (1990). *Social linguistics and literacies: Ideology in discourses.* London, UK: Falmer.

Halliday, M. A. K. (1994). *An introduction to functional grammar* (2nd ed.). London, UK: Edward Arnold.

Halliday, M. A. K. (2003). On language and linguistics. New York, NY: Continuum.

Hart, B., & Risley, R. T. (1995). *Meaningful differences in the everyday experience of young American children.* Baltimore, MD: Paul H. Brookes.

Hinkel, E. (2009). *Teaching academic vocabulary and helping students retain it.* Paper presented at the 43rd Annual TESOL Convention and Exhibit, Denver, CO.

Labov, W. (2006). *Unendangered dialects, endangered people.* Retrieved from http://www.ling.upenn.edu/~wlabov/Papers/UDEP.pdf

Lesaux, N., Koda, K., Seigel, L., & Shanahan, T. (2006). Development of literacy. In D. August & T. Shanahan (Eds.), *Developing literacy in second-language learners: A report of the National Literacy Panel on Language Minority Children and Youth* (pp. 55–122). Mahwah, NJ: Lawrence Erlbaum.

Park, H. M., & Enderle, P. (2006). *Biology: Cycles of life.* Circle Pines, MN: AGS.

Nation, I. S. P. (2001). Learning vocabulary in another language. Cambridge, UK: Cambridge University Press.

Pransky, K. (2008). *Beneath the surface: The hidden realities of teaching culturally and linguistically diverse young learners K–6.* Portsmouth, NH: Heinemann.

Rowling, J. K. (1997). *Harry Potter and the sorcerer's stone.* New York, NY: Scholastic.

Soto-Hinman, I., & Hetzel, J. (2009). *The literacy gaps: Bridge-building strategies for English language learners and standard English learners.* Thousand Oaks, CA: Corwin.

Webb, S. (2007). The effects of repetition on vocabulary knowledge. *Applied Linguistics, 28*(1), 46–65.

Zwiers, J. (2007a). *Building academic language: Essential practices for content classrooms, grades 5–12.* San Francisco: Jossey-Bass.

Zwiers, J. (2007b). *Dimensions and features of academic language.* Retrieved from http://www.jeffzwiers.com/jeffzwiers-com-new_003.htm

Zwiers, J., & Crawford, M. (2011). *Academic conversations: Classroom talk that fosters critical thinking and content understanding.* Portland, ME: Stenhouse.

ENDNOTE

1. A fine source for these mortar words is Appendix B in Zwiers (2007a).

5 Learning as an Academic Process

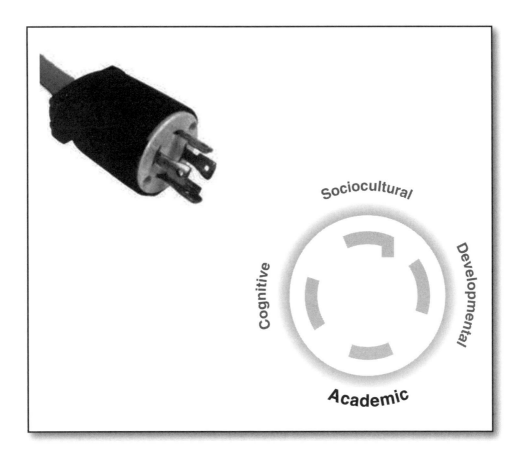

Why is it important to determine key content objectives, what students will do to learn, and the key vocabulary that students will need to use the language of content?

In Chapter 4, we met Eric, an eighth-grade student in Mrs. Shumway's English language arts class. We learned that academic language and literacy learning are a developmental process. In this chapter, we continue our discussion of Mrs. Shumway's work and introduce the third prong of our framework: learning as an academic process. We begin by describing what Mrs. Shumway does to support her students in learning academic content.

As we learned in Chapter 4, Mrs. Shumway is teaming with one of the eighth-grade social studies teachers, Mr. Cantor, to conduct an interdisciplinary unit of study on the Civil War. She has separated her class into four groups, each representing a family that is from either the North or the South and has members who are fighting in the Civil War. Eric's group of four students represents a Southern family.

"What roles have you selected for each member of your group?" Mrs. Shumway asks Eric's small group. One classmate has taken the role of the father, another the mother, a third the sister; Eric has taken the role of the brother who, along with his father, is fighting in the war. His task is to engage in writing letters to his mother and sister, who remain at home. Eric is concerned about his reading and writing abilities.

While Eric knows that he will be engaged in letter writing, to do this task well he must have depth of understanding about the concepts that are being studied, in this case the Civil War, as well as the means to express or communicate this understanding. We might call the former, what it is that Eric will learn, and the latter, what he will do to learn and how he will demonstrate that he has achieved these learning objectives.

In Chapter 3, we discussed the importance of connecting learning to issues that are personally and socially relevant to students' lives. Mrs. Shumway believes that writing personal letters between family members will spark and sustain her students' interest in learning about the Civil War. She plans to connect what students read to socially relevant issues so that they will be invested in learning the concepts. She also believes strongly in pair and group work, as she knows that it provides her students with multiple practice opportunities to use, apply, and learn and use the language of the content that they will be studying. This, too, relates to the importance of the sociocultural frame.

In Chapter 4, we learned that literacy is a developmental process that is highly connected to students' cultural way of being. When literacy practices are not present in a student's culture, teachers must pay focused attention to filling the literacy suitcase to ensure that students are properly equipped. We learned that academic literacy is presented in specific ways according to the genre and subject matter being studied and that students, particularly academic language learners, need to learn how these work. We also learned the critical importance of developing rich vocabulary and some techniques for engaging in this work. Taking all of this into consideration is essential for advancing student achievement.

Determining what is key to learn in terms of the curriculum that is being studied and what students will do to learn it is as critical as the sociocultural and literacy frames. It is the third prong of the four-pronged framework and an important component of the literacy suitcase. It is also the focus of much national attention and certainly a lot of state and local scrutiny. Each state in the nation has curriculum standards. These define the knowledge and skills that must be learned. They are generally separated by subject area and grade level/span and are directly tied to annual state assessments. These assessments are commonly referred to as *high-stakes tests* for two reasons. They are the measures by which teachers and administrators are held accountable for their students' performance, and they are often used to determine whether a student earns a high school diploma (Zacarian, 2011).

One of the largest initiatives occurring in the United States is the Common Core State Standards. They reflect a significant push to create shared benchmarks. The mission of the Standards to

provide a consistent, clear understanding of what students are expected to learn, so teachers and parents know what they need to do to help them. The standards are designed to be robust and relevant to the real world, reflecting the knowledge and skills that our young people need for success in college and careers. With American students fully prepared for the future, our communities will be best positioned to compete successfully in the global economy. (Common Core State Standards Initiative, 2012d, para. 1)

The benchmarks set by states' curriculum standards and/or the Common Core State Standards (2012a) supply us with information about the knowledge that students should possess. However, they do not provide information about how to teach the content or the materials used to teach it. This means that while Mrs. Shumway can go to the standards to determine the knowledge and skills that students should achieve, she cannot expect to secure information about how to ensure that this happens. To create optimal learning environments that are accessible for all learners, we must look to the research on teaching and learning.

DEFINING OVERARCHING OBJECTIVES

One of the most crucial elements in planning and delivering lessons is to determine the key concepts that are absolutely essential for students to learn. Equally important is developing the tasks and activities that students will engage in to learn these concepts. Let's look at the first important element, determining the key concepts. What is it that we want our students to know and be able to do by the end of a unit of study? It is vital to narrow the possibilities down to what is key so that our students can learn.

Gardner (2009) describes the flood of information that is available to us. This is especially true given the capacity in our digital age to secure a huge amount of information with a few keystrokes. For example, at the time of writing this book, I typed the words *Civil War* into Google and received 450 million results! With so much information available to me, how could I possibly choose what is the most relevant? As teachers, we have to help our students understand what is essential in their efforts to achieve the academic goals that we set. Determining an overarching unit or theme objective is paramount for this to occur effectively, as is displaying it for our students.

Let's look at Mrs. Shumway's planning as an example of this synthesizing activity. What does she expect her students to know at the end of their letter-writing activity? She cannot and should not leave this to chance. She first looks closely at the eighth-grade writing section in the Common Core State Standards, the benchmark that her state has adopted. Under the Anchor Standard for writing narratives, it states:

> Write narratives to develop real or imagined experiences or events using effective technique, well-chosen details, and well-structured event sequences. (Common Core State Standards Initiative, 2012b)

As she reads this, she begins to think about what she should post in her classroom for her students to see during the span of this theme-based interdisciplinary unit of study. Displaying overarching unit objectives has been found to be a key element of advancing student achievement (Echevarria, Vogt, & Short, 2002; Wiggins & McTighe, 2005). It underscores the important role that teachers play in planning and delivering lessons. As we do this, it means that we must take into account the goals set by our local and state standards and design tasks and activities that will engage our learners in achieving these goals (Haynes & Zacarian, 2010; Wiggins & McTighe, 2005; Zacarian, 2011). Wiggins and McTighe (2005), nationally recognized educational scholars in curriculum delivery and assessment reform, discuss the importance of thinking backward about our learning goals. By this, they mean the act of thinking carefully and conceptually about what it is that we want students to be able to know and do at the end of a unit of study and then working backward to create tasks and activities that are specifically targeted for achieving these learning goals. To do this we must engage in a paring process to secure the core or essential goals of learning. Gardner (2009) refers to this process as using our synthesizing minds.

A way to explain this task is to describe the steps that Mrs. Shumway takes to define an overarching objective that she crafts to guide her students in this unit of study. In thinking about the unit on the Civil War, she draws from the Common Core writing standards. In looking at them more closely, she notes the following standards about narrative writing for students in the eighth grade.

- Engage and orient the reader by establishing a context and point of view and introducing a narrator and/or characters; organize an event sequence that unfolds naturally and logically.
- Use narrative techniques, such as dialogue, pacing, description, and reflection, to develop experiences, events, and/or characters.
- Use a variety of transition words, phrases, and clauses to convey sequence, signal shifts from one time frame or setting to another, and show the relationships among experiences and events.
- Use precise words and phrases, relevant descriptive details, and sensory language to capture the action and convey experiences and events.
- Provide a conclusion that follows from and reflects on the narrated experiences or events. (Common Core State Standards Initiative, 2012b)

Using this information, Mrs. Shumway then begins to explore the possibilities of how her students might make sense of the time period of the

Civil War through narrative writing. This is where the craft of teaching comes into play, as she has many possibilities for the type of tasks and activities that she can create and deliver. Determining an *essential question* that will guide students in the unit of study is an important first step (Wiggins & McTighe, 2005).

DETERMINING WHAT IS ESSENTIAL

Mrs. Shumway has to think discerningly about one idea that will guide her in the creation of this unit of study. It will also guide her and her students throughout the delivery process. Wiggins and McTighe (2005) discuss the importance of creating an essential question with three specific characteristics:

1. Encourages inquiry and cannot be answered easily

2. Engages learners in the discipline being studied

3. Helps students make sense of what is being studied

To do this, Mrs. Shumway reviews the novel that her students will read, *The Red Badge of Courage* (Crane, 1895), and the chapter in their social studies text on the Civil War. Using the Common Core State Standards, the novel, and social studies text, she then begins to think about the endless possibilities available to her in creating a unit of study and the essential question that she knows is important for her students. Here are two examples of essential questions on other topics:

1. Why is the rainforest important to our planet?

2. Does art reflect society, or does society reflect art?

Mrs. Shumway must consider various essential questions. As a lesson designer, she has found that her students love to use their imagination. She begins to think about the possibilities of personal narrative writing and an essential question that will guide them in this study. She forms the question and begins to think backward from it. An important element as you read this question is whether it will provide access to all of Mrs. Shumway's students, including Eric.

The following reflection prompts have been separated for individual study and team study. Complete the prompt that applies to your particular context.

REFLECTION PROMPT FOR INDIVIDUAL STUDY

Time for Reflection:

Reflect on the following questions, and write responses. Mrs. Shumway developed this essential question for her unit of study: Why are personal letters important for understanding the world in which we live?

- How does this essential question parallel what you have read about the three characteristics of an essential question?

- In what ways is this essential question written in a student-friendly way?

- Create two to three essential questions on a topic of your choosing or that are related to Mrs. Shumway's unit of study.

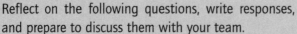

**REFLECTION PROMPT FOR TEAM
STUDY AND OUR-O-LOGUE**

Time for Reflection:

Reflect on the following questions, write responses,
and prepare to discuss them with your team.

Mrs. Shumway developed this essential question for her unit of study: Why are personal letters important for understanding the world in which we live?

- With a partner, define how this question does or does not address the three characteristics of an essential question.

- Visit a classroom, and note how students are made aware of the overarching goals of a unit of study. Are there displays, handouts, or other visual devices that provide an anchor for students to understand the goals of learning? If not, describe how you know what students are learning.

- Look at a course text that includes chapters, headings, subheadings, and so forth. How do these help or not help us in determining an essential question?

- Create a small description of a unit of study, or select one from a standard. Create an overarching essential question that you might use with your students. Bring the description and essential question to your team meeting, and discuss them. Be prepared to receive feedback and/or suggestions for alternative essential questions and to provide teammates with feedback and suggestions as well.

Do you believe that the essential question Mrs. Shumway created will guide her students throughout the unit of study? If she engages her students in imagining that they are family members experiencing the Civil War and writing personal narratives about it, will these tasks and activities help her students respond to the essential question that she has created? Mrs. Shumway asks herself this question by revisiting the standards and the content materials that she plans for her students to read. She also thinks about the possibilities of inviting some guest speakers who have experienced what it is like to either fight in a war or communicate with a loved one who is fighting in a war. She goes back to her essential question and tests it to see whether it can be used to guide her in this planning and delivery cycle. She determines that it will work for her plans.

One of the reflection questions asked about whether her essential question was written in a student-friendly way. When we consider the design and delivery of our lessons, we must consider the ways in which we provide access for everyone. What does this mean? First, we should plan for teaching a diverse group of learners, including academic language learners. But there are many additional reasons for creating clear and explicit essential questions as well. Many classrooms include volunteers, special educators, reading specialists, and others who work with students. Writing a clear, easy-to-read, simply worded essential question opens access to

- our diverse population of learners;
- educators, including reading specialists, special educators, paraprofessionals, and others who work with diverse populations of students;
- parents; and
- supervisors.

In my work with pre- and inservice educators in teacher preparation programs and schools, I have found that many copy and paste their state standard, display it for their students, and refer to it as their overarching objective. I have found it equally commonplace for educators to use sophisticated vocabulary in the overarching objective or essential question. An example of this type of vocabulary and usage is the following essential question:

Why is narrative important for using effective technique, well-chosen details, and well-structured event sequences?

As we learned in Chapter 4, while academic language learners have rich language systems, these do not match school language. A quality essential question is one that is written in accessible, everyday language that all students can understand. The example above does not reflect this type of language. Rather, it presupposes that all of our students and the staff with whom they work, as well as supervisors. have depth of understanding about the following terms, words, and phrases: *narrative, effective technique, well-chosen details,* and *well-structured event sequences.* Using sophisticated language in the essential questions provides access to a certain segment of the student population, those who carry academic language and staff and supervisors who are familiar with technical subject-specific language. It is not as inclusive as it must be. It is imperative that the essential question be written in user-friendly language to provide access for all of our students, their parents, the staff with whom they work, and instructional leaders.

DEFINING THE DAY'S LEARNING OBJECTIVES

Determining and displaying the day's learning objective are equally important. What is meant by a day's learning objective? It is what students will know by the end of a specific lesson. A learning objective should be created for each lesson and presented and visually displayed in addition to a unit's essential question (Echevarria et al., 2002). Its purpose is to provide a clear idea of what it is that that will be learned. A learning objective plays a number of key roles that are similar to a unit's essential question. Forming and displaying clear, easy-to-read, simply worded learning objectives for each lesson also opens access to our diverse population of learners and their families, the staff who work with them, and instructional leaders. To determine learning objectives, we must review the same process we did to form essential questions. Let's look at one of Mrs. Shumway's lessons to see how she developed the learning objective.

Mrs. Shumway reviews the Common Core writing standards, one of which includes the following:

> Engage and orient the reader by establishing a context and point of view and introducing a narrator and/or characters; organize an event sequence that unfolds naturally and logically. (Common Core State Standards Initiative, 2012c)

Knowing that she wants her students to write letters to and from family members, Mrs. Shumway thinks about the ways in which they might be able to describe the context of the Civil War, a particular family's point of view about it, and a sequence of events as they unfold. One means for doing this would be to ask her students to work in their groups and discuss the reasons why a someone would choose to fight in the Civil War and what this might have meant to his family members. She also thinks about the ways in which the context can be explained and reviews the two texts that her students will be reading, their social studies text and *The Red Badge of Courage* (Crane, 1895).

Literacy is connected to four domains: listening, speaking, reading, and writing. As teachers, we often think of reading and writing as the academic side of literacy. However, listening and speaking are truly essential connection makers. They connect speaking to writing and listening to reading. For this to occur, we have to consider how to make this an active process. In a real sense, the type of linguistic mentorship that Soto-Hinman and Hetzel (2009) advocate reflects this type of thinking. Actively engaging students in practicing what they will write by first talking about it is important, and the same is true for engaging students in listening to read. Let's look at what Mrs. Shumway does to reflect this type of mentorship.

In the opening chapter of *The Red Badge of Courage*, we learn that the main character voluntarily left home, joined a regiment, and is waiting to go into battle. We also learn that he has many feelings about leaving his mother and worries about whether he is ready for battle. Will he run away? Will he be able to face his enemy? These are key questions that he asks himself. The opening chapter of the textbook (Appleby, Brinkley, Broussard, McPherson, & Ritchie, 2009) is filled with information on various topics, including a short comparison of the North and South, Confederate and Union strategies, and an economic timeline perspective of the salaries that soldiers earned between the Civil War in the 1860s and the Iraq War in 2007. With so much information, how can Mrs. Shumway and Mr. Cantor create lessons that will be comprehensible and doable for their students and include daily learning objectives?

Mrs. Shumway returns to her essential question: *Why are personal letters important for understanding the world in which we live?* She also revisits the Common Core State Standards and confers with Mr. Cantor about the content and the key vocabulary that will be covered in his social studies class. These guide her thinking about how to create explicit listening, speaking, reading, and writing activities that are targeted to the standards. She is always seeking ways to connect her essential question and the culminating activity that she has created with the daily lessons. Using this backward design, she begins to assemble a series of activities that her students will do throughout the unit of study. Each activity includes a specific learning goal that Mrs. Shumway will display. She will refer to these and the essential unit question routinely throughout the unit of study. Now let's look at another feature of a lesson plan and delivery: the activities that students will do to learn or what they will do to listen, speak, read, and write.

WHAT STUDENTS WILL DO TO LEARN

Academic literacy includes four methods of communication. We listen, speak, read, and write. To communicate well and to carry academic language means that we must be competent in each of these domains. While we might call these "do" activities, the research about these is more commonly referred to as *language objectives* (Echevarria et al., 2002). These help to guide students in what they will be engaging in to learn. Rather than use the state standards, which are often written in technical teacher language, it is important to include short, easily accessible statements about what students will do to learn in the day's language objectives. It is critical that these connect what students will do to communicate in the content that they are studying.

What is critical about language objectives is that they must be targeted to ensure active participation. Mrs. Shumway plans to read aloud the first chapter of the novel. The following reflection activity is intended to help in determining what might be an active activity and what might be a passive activity.

The following reflection prompts have been separated for individual study and team study. Complete the prompt that applies to your particular context.

REFLECTION PROMPT FOR INDIVIDUAL STUDY

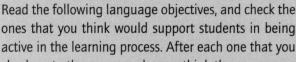

Time for Reflection:

Read the following language objectives, and check the ones that you think would support students in being active in the learning process. After each one that you check, note the reasons why you think these are more active than passive.

- Listen to the first chapter of *The Red Badge of Courage,* and discuss it.

- Pay attention to Henry's feelings about leaving home, and comment on two of his feelings with a partner.

(Continued)

(Continued)

- Focus on Henry's fears about fighting in the war, and report on two of his feelings with a partner.

- Listen to a story about when Henry leaves his home to fight in the Civil War, and discuss it.

REFLECTION PROMPT FOR TEAM STUDY AND OUR-O-LOGUE

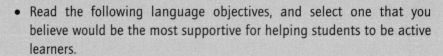

Time for Reflection:

Reflect on the following questions, write responses, and prepare to discuss them with your team.

- Read the following language objectives, and select one that you believe would be the most supportive for helping students to be active learners.

  o Each group should engage in a Round Robin Read-Aloud of the first chapter of *The Red Badge of Courage.*
  o Read the first chapter of *The Red Badge of Courage.*

    ○ Listen to a story about when Henry leaves home to fight in the Civil War, jot down two to three feelings that he has about it, and discuss these with a partner.

- Discuss three to four reasons why you made this particular selection.

- Based on your reasoning, create a learning task and describe it. Create a language objective for this task. Discuss these ideas with your group.

It is critical that students engage in activities that are targeted for the outcomes that we envision. In the prior individual reflection activity, the first and last examples do not require students to pay focused attention or engage in actions for a specific purpose. The second and third examples are focused and intentional. They also engage students in activities that are targeted for listening-to-read and speaking-to-write activities. Language objectives can most easily begin with an action verb. Figure 5.1 provides examples of intentional activities for listening, speaking, reading, and writing:

Figure 5.1 Action Verb Suggestions for Creating Objectives

Listening	Speaking	Reading	Writing
Listen for . . .	Retell two things . . .	Look for . . .	Write about these specific ideas . . .
Look for . . .	Comment on one idea . . .	Read for . . .	Compare . . . with . . .
Pay attention to . . .	Persuade your partner using two arguments . . .	Sequence the story into . . .	Describe the place that . . .
Focus on . . .	Present one idea . . .	Identify . . .	Create a timeline of . . .
Concentrate on . . .	Report on . . .	Find information about . . .	Draw conclusions by . . .

EXPLICIT VOCABULARY INSTRUCTION/DEVELOPMENT

Academic or content vocabulary is essential for students who carry academic language and academic language learners. In Chapter 4, we discussed Tier 1, 2, and 3 vocabulary as described by Beck, McKeown, and Kucan (2002). In this chapter, we will focus more closely on Tier 3 vocabulary, which includes terms, words, idioms, and phrases (TWIPs) that are likely to be found in classroom settings and course texts. They are also often multisyllabic and are not likely to be spoken or used outside of the classroom. In terms of Mrs. Shumway's unit, they include examples such as *Confederacy, Emancipation Proclamation, tributary, casualty,* and *ironclad.* All students need instruction in these words. A distinction between students who carry academic language and academic language learners is that it may take as many as 12 to 15 active practice opportunities for academic language learners to learn and be able to use them at will (Hinkel, 2009).

A word of caution: Providing students with multiple active practice and exposure opportunities to use vocabulary to the point of mastery should be fundamental to our work. However, research has shown that this type of instruction is not routine (Francis, Rivera, Lesaux, Kieffer, & Rivera, 2006). What is missing is frequency of active practice opportunities that are meaningful and purposeful. Authentic opportunities to use words in context and in the text structure in which they are found should be a mainstay in our classes. Visuals such as drawings of the vocabulary (Marzano & Pickering, 2005) and categorized word walls (Haynes & Zacarian, 2010; Zacarian, 2011), as well as student practice using the vocabulary in context (Blachowicz & Fisher, 2004), are essential.

Mrs. Shumway posts a word wall of Tier 3 English language arts vocabulary that is essential for her students to learn. Mr. Cantor does the same. While their interdisciplinary word walls are complementary, they reflect the content of their specific subject matter. Mrs. Shumway includes vocabulary from the novel, and Mr. Cantor the course text. In both cases, they think carefully about the volume of TWIPs that they display and expect their students to learn. Course books, including the novel and text that Mrs. Shumway and Mr. Cantor use, are chock-full of content-specific vocabulary, and students do not need to learn all of it. We must think carefully about the actual academic TWIPs that are needed and synthesize these down to what is essential.

In addition, we must help our students begin to strategically analyze words for their meanings. This can involve separating words that they know from words that they do not know and looking for similarities or context cues among the latter. Taking time to do this is essential. Pransky (2008) uses the phrase *death words* to define what happens to students when they do not understand important vocabulary. He uses this in reference to what he believes happens—it kills meaning or comprehension. Teaching students to use word analysis processes, such as looking for similar prefixes and using context clues by building on students' background to help build the capacity to make a strategic or educated guess, can greatly help students build their academic vocabulary (Zwiers, 2007).

PUTTING THE ACADEMIC FRAME INTO PRACTICE

Use clear, overarching learning and language objectives for the unit and the day

- Define and display clearly articulated unit objectives and the day's learning and language objectives in student-friendly language.
- Direct student attention to the unit and day's learning and language objectives at the beginning of, during, and at the end of the lesson.
- Provide language goals that reflect what students will do to learn (i.e., the process of learning) and how they will communicate what they have learned (learning product).

(Continued)

(Continued)

Provide explicit vocabulary instruction

- Post key content vocabulary in organized ways.
- Provide multiple opportunities for students to practice using vocabulary in academic conversation (i.e., content terms, words, idioms, and phrases) in order to "own" it.

Provide challenging activities

- Design and enact challenging activities with clear standards/expectations and performance feedback.
- Assist students in developing more complex thinking by engaging them in academic conversations (using pair and small-group work) that require using the language of content.

Provide modeling and practice opportunities

- Provide a model of a completed product that students then make.
- Model the behavior, thinking processes, or procedures necessary for the task, and assist students during practice.
- Provide multiple and frequent practice opportunities for students to learn the content.

SUMMARY

In this chapter, we discussed the importance of drawing from state, district, and/or local standards to determine what is key for students to learn. We looked at the importance of defining the key unit and day's learning objectives and displaying these in student-friendly, accessible language. We discussed the importance of using this same kind of language in creating communication objectives for what students will do to learn. Finally, we described the significance of graphically displaying well-organized, subject-specific word walls.

Helping students think as learners is key for advancing their achievement, and we will explore this process in Chapter 6.

REFERENCES

Appleby, J., Brinkley, A., Broussard, A. S., McPherson, J. M., & Ritchie, D. A. (2009). *The American journey.* Columbus, OH: Glencoe/McGraw-Hill.

Beck, I., McKeown, M. G., & Kucan, L. (2002). *Bringing words to life: Robust vocabulary instruction.* New York, NY: Guilford Press.

Blachowicz, C. L. Z., & Fisher, P. (2004). Keeping the "fun" in fundamental: Encouraging word awareness and incidental word learning in the classroom through word play. In J. F. Baumann & E. J. Kame'enui (Eds.), *Vocabulary instruction: Research to practice* (pp. 218–238). New York, NY: Guilford Press.

Common Core State Standards Initiative. (2012a). *About the standards.* Retrieved from http://www.corestandards.org/about-the-standards

Common Core State Standards Initiative. (2012b). *English language arts standards, anchor standards, college and career readiness anchor standards for writing.* Retrieved from http://www.corestandards.org/the-standards/english-language-arts-standards/anchor-standards-6–12/college-and-career-readiness-anchor-standards-for-writing/

Common Core State Standards Initiative. (2012c). *English language arts standards, writing, grade 8.* Retrieved from http://www.corestandards.org/the-standards/english-language-arts-standards/writing-6–12/grade-8/

Common Core State Standards Initiative. (2012d). *Mission statement.* Retrieved from http://www.corestandards.org/

Crane, S. (1895). *The red badge of courage.* New York, NY: D. Appleton.

Echevarria, J., Vogt, M. E., & Short, D. (2002). *The SIOP model: Sheltered instruction for academic achievement.* Washington, DC: Center for Applied Linguistics.

Francis, D. J., Rivera, M., Lesaux, N., Kieffer, M., & Rivera, J. (2006). *Practical guidelines for the education of English language learners: Research-based recommendations for instruction and academic interventions.* Portsmouth, NH: RMC Research Corporation, Center on Instruction.

Gardner, H. (2009). *Five minds for the future.* Cambridge, MA: Harvard University Press.

Haynes, J., & Zacarian, D. (2010). *Teaching English language learners across the content areas.* Alexandria, VA: Association for Supervision and Curriculum Development.

Hinkel, E. (2009). *Teaching academic vocabulary and helping students retain it.* Paper presented at the 43rd Annual TESOL Convention and Exhibit, Denver, CO.

Marzano, R. J., & Pickering, D. J. (2005). *Building academic vocabulary: Teacher's manual.* Alexandria, VA: Association for Supervision and Curriculum Development.

Pransky, K. (2008). *Beneath the surface: The hidden realities of teaching culturally and linguistically diverse young learners K–6.* Portsmouth, NH: Heinemann.

Soto-Hinman, I., & Hetzel, J. (2009). *The literacy gaps: Bridge-building strategies for English language learners and standard English learners.* Thousand Oaks, CA: Corwin.

Wiggins, G. T., & McTighe, J. (2005). *Understanding by design* (expanded 2nd ed.). Alexandria, VA: Association for Supervision and Curriculum Development.

Zacarian, D. (2011). *Tranforming schools for English learners: A comprehensive guide for school leaders.* Thousand Oaks, CA: Corwin.

Zwiers, J. (2007). *Building academic language: Essential practices for content classrooms, grades 5–12.* San Francisco, CA: Jossey-Bass.

6 Learning as a Cognitive Process

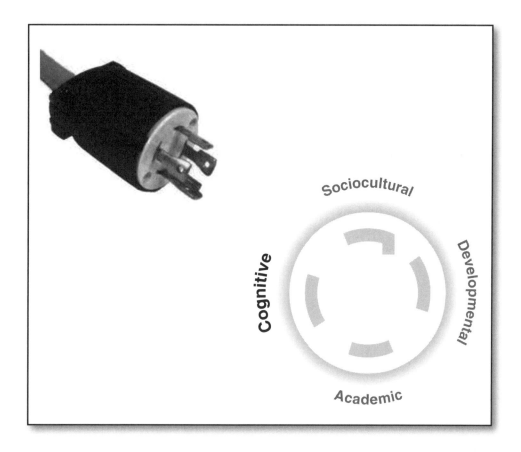

Why is it critical to teach students how to think to learn?

We begin our discussion about the importance of teaching students how to think to learn by visiting Mrs. Nelson's fourth-grade social studies class, where we meet one of her students, Benjamin.

Benjamin is a student in Mrs. Nelson's fourth-grade class. The class is working on a social studies unit on recent African immigrant groups. On the board in the front of the classroom is a list of the various immigrant groups and their countries of origin. Above the list, Mrs. Nelson has written an essential question to guide this unit of study: *Why is it important to understand the people who live in our community?* She has placed a map of Africa on the board and magnetic tacks on the countries that she has selected for her class to study. Attached to these tacks are pieces of string that connect to notes, photos, and symbols that she has pasted onto the wall. They describe various climate and geographic regions in Africa, languages that people speak, areas that have experienced civil strife, and more.

Mrs. Nelson tells her class that they will be separated into small groups and that each group will be assigned a particular immigrant group. She reviews the materials that she has posted on the wall, including the various countries, their geographic region, and other details that she has labeled. With the small space that is left on the board, she writes the numbers 1, 2, and 3, and as she describes each of three tasks, she points to the associated number that she has written on the board. She tells each small group that their task is to describe the home country that each group has been assigned, the reasons why its people came to the United States, and the locations in the United States where the majority have settled.

Benjamin's group will study Ethiopians. Before moving into his group, he raises his hand and is called on by Mrs. Nelson. Here is their exchange:

Benjamin: Are Ethiopians American?

Mrs. Nelson: They're immigrants from Ethiopia who come to the United States.

Benjamin: They're not American?

Mrs. Nelson: They are people who move from Ethiopia to live in the United States permanently, you know, for the rest of their lives.

Benjamin: Oh.

Thus far, Benjamin has listened to and observed Mrs. Nelson carefully and taken notes. Figure 6.1 depicts what he has written in his notebook. When Mrs. Nelson separates her class into small learning groups, Benjamin grabs his notebook and brings it to his group.

Figure 6.1   Benjamin's Notes

Ethiopians		
Description of home country	**Reasons they came to the United States**	**Where the majority live in the United States**
	Live their lives	

The following reflection prompts have been separated for individual study and team study. Complete the prompt that applies to your particular context.

REFLECTION PROMPT FOR INDIVIDUAL STUDY

Time for Reflection:

Reflect on the following question, and write a response.

- Describe three to four reasons why you think Benjamin is or is not prepared to engage in his group's task.

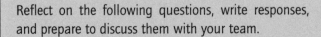

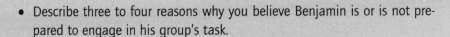

REFLECTION PROMPT FOR TEAM STUDY AND OUR-O-LOGUE

Time for Reflection:

Reflect on the following questions, write responses, and prepare to discuss them with your team.

- Describe three to four reasons why you believe Benjamin is or is not prepared to engage in his group's task.

- Observe a student who is engaging in a small-group task. Note the task that the student is asked to do. Describe interactions that the student engages in with his or her small group. Compare these with your discussion about Benjamin.

One of the major skills that Benjamin possesses, among others, is his ability to understand the task at hand. A second skill is his ability to begin to engage in the learning task independently.

In Figure 6.2, we see the close proximity between the box denoting the assigned task and the box representing the ability to engage in it successfully. There is almost no separation between the two. They sit closely together, signifying the lack or very limited amount of scaffolding or direct supports that Benjamin needs to engage in the learning task.

Figure 6.2 Benjamin's Skills

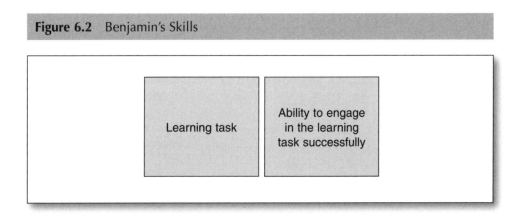

Figure 6.3 Gap Between the Task and Engagement in It

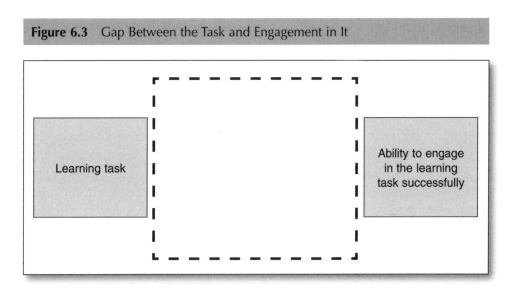

Figure 6.3 presents us with a different depiction of the relationship between the learning task and the ability to engage in it successfully. The two sit completely apart from each other, and nested between them is a large blank box. For some students, the blank box represents a lack of capacity to engage in classwork successfully without much-needed supports. Direct teaching of thinking-to-learn skills must fill this middle space, or vacuum.

An important question for us to ask ourselves is: How do we create learning environments in which all students, especially academic language learners, can clearly understand the task and engage in it? In other words, what needs to occur to bring the two boxes illustrated in Figure 6.4 closer and closer together? To begin this discussion, let's look closely at learning as a cognitive or thinking-to-learn process.

Figure 6.4 Thinking-to-Learn Skills Needed to Engage in a Task Successfully

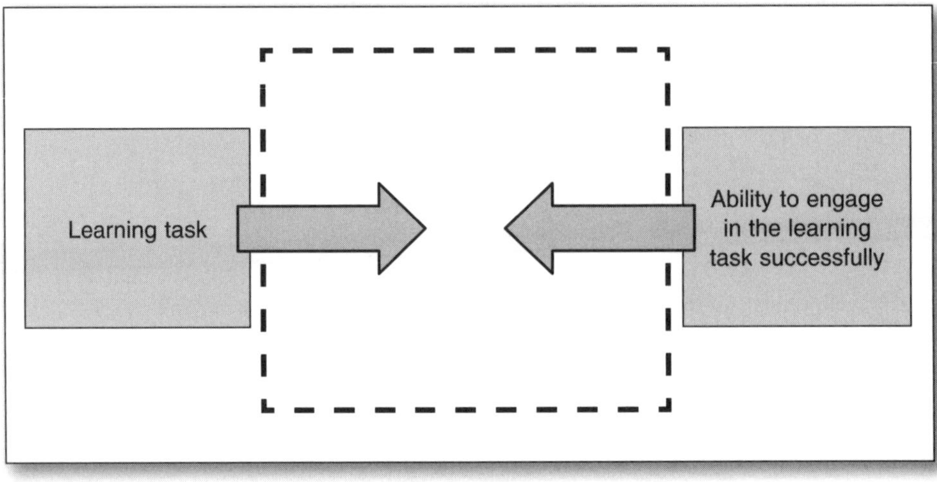

THINKING TO LEARN

When we think about something, we engage in a focused process. For example, as Benjamin thought about his small group's assignment, he took in all of the information that Mrs. Nelson presented to the whole class, thought carefully about the task that she assigned, separated it into three categories, and created a chart that helped him visually depict the task. The thinking process that he engaged is not simple. Cognitive psychologists Feuerstein, Feuerstein, and Falik (2010) tell us that we are confronted with more stimuli in a single day than early man experienced during the span of a lifetime!

Mrs. Nelson provides her students with a load of facts and images about African immigrant groups. Her classroom is filled with visual information and artifacts about different African countries and their people. However, with all of this information confronting Benjamin, he is skillfully able to sift through what is needed to begin engaging in the learning task. In this sense, he is able to pull together the two boxes depicted in Figure 6.4.

He has capably begun to think about what is to be learned, but thinking is not something that is accomplished independently. While this might sound strange, we have to look closely at what constitutes thinking. Many of us are familiar with Vygotsky's theories about cognition. Briefly, Vygotsky (1978) proposes that learning is an interactive process that is socially constructed. We learn through interacting with our external world.

Further, we construct meaning from what we experience. That is to say that we must be active participants in our own development, and we use what we learn from our environment to develop the tools that we need to think (Rogoff, 1990).

The following reflection prompts have been separated for individual study and team study. Complete the prompt that applies to your particular context.

REFLECTION PROMPT FOR INDIVIDUAL STUDY

Time for Reflection:

Reflect on the following questions, and write responses.

- Describe a situation in which you learned by participating in an interaction.

- Drawing from this situation, describe what you did to learn.

**REFLECTION PROMPT FOR TEAM
STUDY AND OUR-O-LOGUE**

Time for Reflection:

Reflect on the following question, write a response,
and prepare to discuss it with your team.

- With a partner, share three to four ways in which interactions helps each
  of you learn.

NEGOTIATING MEANING

We also use language to wrestle with ideas that we are considering and to
make meaning of them. In the exchange between Benjamin and Mrs. Nelson,
we can see that Benjamin is not clear on the definition of an immigrant.
Mrs. Nelson works with him to help him understand the concept. Michael
Long (1983) defines this type of exchange as one in which participants
negotiate meaning. While this concept is commonly referenced in the literature about second language acquisition, it is an important means for
describing how meaning is made or thinking to learn is accomplished
through interaction.

Babies typically interact actively with parents, siblings, or caregivers
and learn through these interactive negotiating experiences. Following
this train of thought, carriers of academic language engage in thinking-to-
learn activities from a young age and carry these into school. Academic
language learners need to be supported in these activities. While at times,
we might feel that the gaps between students who carry academic language and academic language learners is too large to close, we should
never think that it is impossible, especially in light of our capacity, as
humans, to change. One of the most important factors in the transforma-
tion from an academic language learner to a carrier of academic language

is that it must be an active process. Let's look at an example when only some students are actively engaged.

In this example, Mrs. Nelson has separated her fourth-grade social studies class into small groups. Benjamin is eager to share his thoughts with his group. He loves to talk and has a lot to say. If Mrs. Nelson observes Benjamin in his small group, she will see that he dominates the talk and that this behavior prevents the other group members from participating. This type of behavior is a common occurrence in classrooms across our country. Some students dominate the talk, while others sit passively.

THINKING AS AN ACTIVE PROCESS

Thinking to learn is an active process. It requires students to practice or apprentice by using the language of content. Helping all students think about what they are studying by talking about it deeply is the heart of what it means to think to learn. It requires us to create spaces in which *everyone* is active in the process of engaging in course content.

Benjamin is adept at making meaning of the resources that Mrs. Nelson has made available to him. Further, as a carrier of academic language he has been conditioned in this process. He understands what is required of him. He knows what Mrs. Nelson is conveying. Also, he is skilled at how to use academic language to express his understanding. Let's look at the skills that he possesses.

Michael Halliday (1993), a renowned sociolinguist, theorizes that we reflect on our own language resources to achieve understanding, and we build and adapt our knowledge base through interaction. The process requires that we be deeply familiar with members of our learning community. Gee (1990) defines this type of membership as being someone who understands the language discourse.[1] To be an active learner requires that we understand the implied rules, systems, and codes of our learning community. Carriers of academic language, such as Benjamin, already possess this type of discourse, whereas academic language learners must be explicitly apprenticed into it.

Let's look at an example of implied classroom discourse. Two courses that I taught at the University of Massachusetts (Managing Culturally Responsive Classrooms and Developing Curriculum for the Heterogeneous) were designed to foster pre- and inservice educators' thinking about carriers of academic language and academic language learners. In each, graduate students engaged in observation and interactive tasks in authentic classrooms. One year, many of the graduate students engaged in these tasks in kindergarten settings. In these, we noted that the kindergarten teachers used nonverbal signals to convey three messages: *stop doing what you are doing, listen to my command,* and *transition to the next activity.* Nonverbal examples of these signals included a raised hand known as a "stop sign," lights flicked on and off, and the rhythmic clapping of hands. In a few, the command "Look and listen" accompanied one of the nonverbal signals.

In these kindergarten settings, it looked as if each student understood the nonverbal and verbal/nonverbal commands. We noted that the children stopped and looked at their teachers and appeared to listen to them. However, we wanted to see if what we thought we observed meant that the students understood what was demanded of them. Unfortunately, we found that many did not know that the signal conveyed the three intended messages. Subgroups, including English learners and students whom the kindergarten teachers identified as "struggling to learn," understood the signal as meaning only the first of the three intended messages—stop or freeze.

So while thinking to learn is a process, we have to consider how to remedy the differences between carriers of academic language and academic language learners. To a great degree, it involves making what we say and do explicit, visible, and understood. This is what is needed to disrupt the educational inequalities that exist between carriers of academic language and academic language learners.

Figure 6.5 describes a couple of the remedying elements, including helping students understand the meaning of the language task. In the kindergarten example provided earlier, some of the students understood the coded meaning of the nonverbal signals, and others did not.

Figure 6.5 Disrupting Educational Inequalities

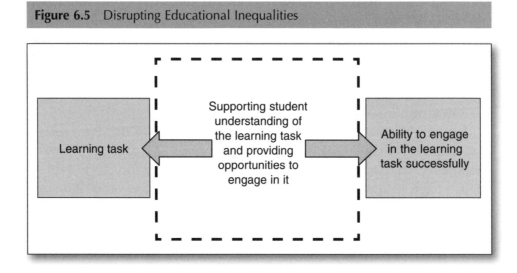

Learning task

Supporting student understanding of the learning task and providing opportunities to engage in it

Ability to engage in the learning task successfully

To remedy this inequality, students must *crack the code* to *break into* and subsequently use the language of school (Wells, 1994). This can only happen by engaging students in two types of activities. First, explicitly support their understanding of a learning task. Second, engage them in using the language of content authentically and enough to be able to use it at will. To do this requires that we provide them with many practice opportunities.

The following reflection prompts have been separated for individual study and team study. Complete the prompt that applies to your particular context.

REFLECTION PROMPT FOR INDIVIDUAL STUDY

Time for Reflection:

Reflect on the following questions, and write responses.

- Observe a classroom setting (it can be your own). Note the language that is used to engage students in a learning task. It can be verbal, nonverbal, or both. Write the language example here.

- Note the ways in which your example reflects the implied rules that reflect classroom discourse.

REFLECTION PROMPT FOR TEAM STUDY AND OUR-O-LOGUE

Time for Reflection:

Reflect on the following questions, write responses, and prepare to discuss them with your team.

- Observe two classroom situations in which students are assigned a task. Describe the ways in which the task is or is not made explicit.

- Discuss two to three actions that might have been included to make the task more explicit.

CRACKING THE CODE TO THINK TO LEARN

As educators, we use many visuals like the ones that Mrs. Nelson uses to support learning. These include her posting an essential question to guide her unit of study as well as the map of Africa and the accompanying notes, symbols, and pictures that she has tacked to the map to make the content more accessible. She also uses group work to help support her students as they engage in the learning tasks. While these are all essential for learning and we discussed many conventions for using them in the earlier chapters of this book, teaching students how to think to learn is also foundational to our work. To do this requires that we identify the language that is needed to perform thinking tasks and to make it visible for our students.

Michael Halliday (1973, 1985, 1993) introduced the idea that we use language to perform different functions. Drawing from his ideas, Peregoy and Boyle (2008) explain how language functions work in classroom settings. According to Peregoy and Boyle's interpretation of Halliday, we use language to do the following:

1. Ask questions; ask for something

2. Tell others what to do, control a situation, determine the sequence of events, and engage in a role-play that requires a level of authority or control

3. Work in pairs and groups

4. Express our feelings or personal experiences

5. Gain knowledge about the world in which we live through questions and explanation of ideas

6. Be creative using our imagination

7. Convey facts and information

If we are to look at what is required in classroom settings, each of these language functions is critical. We must make these functions explicit with the tasks that we require of students. We must also use a variety of tasks and assignments to ensure that we cover the full complement of language functions in our work. How does this work in practice? Many teachers draw from Bloom's taxonomy for understanding the different types of thinking skills that our students need to learn (Anderson & Krathwohl, 2001; Bloom, 1956) These include six categories of increasing levels of cognitive demand:.

1. Remembering

2. Understanding

3. Applying

4. Analyzing

5. Evaluating

6. Creating

Consider what we say to communicate what we remember about an event. It calls for an expression of facts and information. This type of language function requires certain ways of communicating in classroom settings. Mrs. Nelson requires her students to engage in this type of language function in the tasks of requiring students to describe the home country of the African immigrant group that they were assigned and requiring students to describe the U.S. locations where the majority settled. For her students to complete this task successfully, they have to do more than remember facts and information. They have to express their understanding.

The following reflection prompts have been separated for individual study and team study. Complete the prompt that applies to your particular context.

REFLECTION PROMPT FOR INDIVIDUAL STUDY

Time for Reflection:

Reflect on the following question, and write a response.

- Review Peregoy and Boyle's (2008) list of classroom language functions. Think about the tasks that Mrs. Nelson has assigned and the methods that she uses. Identify and list all of the language functions that you think are required of her students: (1) describe the home country that each group has been assigned, (2) explain why people from this country came to the United States, and (3) describe the U.S. locations where the majority settled.

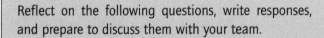

**REFLECTION PROMPT FOR TEAM
STUDY AND OUR-O-LOGUE**

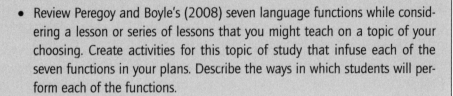

Time for Reflection:

Reflect on the following questions, write responses,
and prepare to discuss them with your team.

- Review Peregoy and Boyle's (2008) seven language functions while considering a lesson or series of lessons that you might teach on a topic of your
  choosing. Create activities for this topic of study that infuse each of the
  seven functions in your plans. Describe the ways in which students will perform each of the functions.

- Review Bloom's categories of cognitive demand. Describe the categories
  that your lesson(s) include.

Requiring students to describe an event may include such important
expression-of-understanding skills as *describe, illustrate, detail,* and *report.* One
of the tasks Mrs. Nelson asked of her students was to explain the reasons
why their African immigrant group left their home country. This calls for a
very different set of language expression skills, such as *summarize, analyze,*
and *explain.* Identifying the language function and the language that students

will use to engage in a thinking-to-learn task is an essential must-do. It is also important to explicitly teach the language that will be used to express content and to provide students with ample opportunities to use it in practice.

DISPLAYING SENTENCE PROMPTS AND RESPONSES TO ENGAGE IN ACADEMIC TALK

Zwiers (2012) provides us with helpful sentence prompts and sentence response starters to apply these ideas in practice. Table mats, white boards, and other devices can be used to illustrate these sentence prompts. They help students engage in what Zwiers calls an *academic conversation* about what they are studying. He aptly states, "Talk is priceless." He has found that helping students engage in meaningful academic conversations about the content that is being studied helps their understanding and oral expressive skills. In turn, it greatly helps their reading and writing skills because they have used the language, have learned how it works in an academic setting, and can move more seamlessly from oral language to text.

These oral academic discussion practice opportunities are essential for building students' thinking-to-learn abilities. This process requires authentic engagement in using academic language in classroom discourse. Individual words, such as vocabulary lists and word walls, are not as helpful as is an academic conversation that uses these words in context. Engaging in an academic conversation is a much more authentic means for thinking to learn and learning to think (Zwiers, 2007). Providing sentence prompts and sentence response starters to start an academic content conversation, according to Zwiers (2012), is a great means for getting students to engage in an academic conversation. Let's look at some sentence prompts and sentence response starters that Mrs. Nelson might require of her students in their group discussion about their African immigrant group (Figure 6.6).

Figure 6.6 Mrs. Nelson's Sentence Prompts and Sentence Response Starters

Prompts

- Can you give an example describing the country from the text?
- Where does it say that?
- What are examples from other texts or our classroom?
- Can you give an example that illustrates the climate of the country?
- Where does it say that?

Responses

- For example, . . .
- In the text, it said that . . .
- One illustration of this is . . .

These would be created into a tablemat or hand out for each group to use, or they would be written on the board. Regardless which means you use, the sentence prompts and response starters must be displayed for students to see.

The following reflection prompts have been separated for individual study and team study. Complete the prompt that applies to your particular context.

REFLECTION PROMPT FOR INDIVIDUAL STUDY

Time for Reflection:

Reflect on the following question, and write a response.

- Create your own sentence prompt and sentence response starters for Mrs. Nelson's activity requiring students to explain the reasons why an African immigrant group came to the United States.

  o Sentence prompt:

  o Sentence response starter:

REFLECTION PROMPT FOR TEAM STUDY AND OUR-O-LOGUE

Time for Reflection:

Reflect on the following question, write a response, and prepare to discuss it with your team.

- With a partner, create two sentence prompts and two sentence response starters for Mrs. Nelson's activity requiring students to explain the reasons why an African immigrant group came to the United States.

  o Sentence prompts:

  o Sentence response starters:

A number of helpful activities, such as these sentence prompts and sentence response starters, can be used for a variety of thinking-to-learn skills. Pair work is a fine means for helping every student practice using this language authentically. A couple of other interesting devices that Zwiers (2012) uses are sentence prompts and sentence responses for *same/different, agree/disagree,* and *for/against.* He uses the same format of sentence prompts and sentence response starters. One student is the director, and the other the speaker. A speaker begins an academic discussion strand by taking a particular stance. The director's clap of a hand or other signal requires the speaker to take an opposing position. Here is an example:

Reasons why an African immigrant group left Africa:

- I believe that African immigrants came here because . . .

Reasons why members of the same African group might not have left Africa:

- On the other hand, they might have stayed in Africa because . . .

Developing and using sentence prompts and sentence response starters provides students with a visual anchor to see how academic language is used (Jensen, 2005).

USING GRAPHIC ORGANIZERS

Graphic organizers are also key anchors for helping students think as learners. While they are commonly used, we often use different ones to mean the same thing. For example, let's say that I ask you to draw a graphic organizer depicting U.S. history events that occurred between 2000 and 2010. Some of us might draw the visual seen in Figure 6.7.

Figure 6.7 Example of Time Span Visual

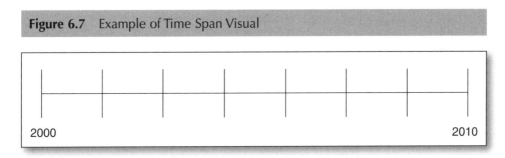

Some of us might draw the visual seen in Figure 6.8.

Figure 6.8 Additional Example of Time Span Visual

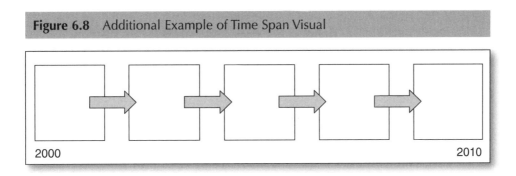

The following reflection prompts have been separated for individual study and team study. Complete the prompt that applies to your particular context.

REFLECTION PROMPT FOR INDIVIDUAL STUDY

Time for Reflection:

Reflect on the following question, and write a response.

- Create your own visual depicting the time span between 2000 and 2010 that is different from Figures 6.7 and 6.8.

REFLECTION PROMPT FOR TEAM STUDY AND OUR-O-LOGUE

Time for Reflection:

Reflect on the following questions, write responses, and prepare to discuss them with your team.

- Create your own visual depicting the time span between 2000 and 2010 that is different from Figures 6.7 and 6.8.

> • Create two visuals that might be used to depict the concept of *same/different.*

While we can draw from our personal experience, creativity, course texts, and the Internet for examples of graphic organizers, we have to think carefully about the variety that we use to depict the same idea. Using various organizers to mean the same thing can be confusing for some students. This is especially true when one student has different teachers or when the same teacher uses different organizers. While our intent is to make ideas more visible, we may lose students who don't have a solid grasp of what each organizer means.

Hyerle (2004) states that we use visual organizers to express eight thinking concepts:

1. Brainstorming

2. Describing

3. Sequencing/ordering

4. Comparing/contrasting

5. Classifying/grouping

6. Describing whole-part relationships

7. Describing cause-effect relationships

8. Seeing analogies

Using the same visual organizer to support students' thinking can greatly help them create a visual map of a concept. It requires that we explicitly teach students about each graphic organizer that we use and how to use it. We should not expect students to understand what we mean without an explicit explanation and without ample practice opportunities to use these visuals authentically.

A word of caution about visual organizers and sentence prompts and sentence response starters. They cannot simply be written on a board, table mat, or handout. As professionals, we have to understand that we must engage students in identifying the sentence prompt, sentence response starter, and graphic organizer that we are using and what we are using it to do. We must also provide students with several examples for using these items. This should include *think-alouds* for how it is used in the context and content being studied. We have to provide students, especially academic language learners, with many opportunities to practice using these devices to learn. It can also be greatly helpful to display the graphic organizers and sentence prompts and sentence response starters that we will use throughout our classrooms so that students have the continuous opportunity to see and use them. Further, it is important to work with general classroom, resource, and specialist educators at all grade levels and across disciplines to collaboratively agree on routine graphic organizers and sentence prompts and sentence response starters. The more students see these visuals in action, the more opportunity they have to apprentice in the language of content to think to learn and, hopefully, internalize and carry it for future use. When this occurs effectively, students are mentored into carrying academic language and have a much greater opportunity for using it at will and adapting it for future use.

PUTTING THE COGNITIVE FRAME INTO PRACTICE

Provide cognitive skill development to understand how we use language to express thinking

- Thinking skills that students need are intentionally taught within the content and activities and draw from students' background knowledge.
- Students are engaged across all levels of Bloom's taxonomy (remembering, understanding, applying, analyzing, evaluating, and creating).
- Students are engaged in Halliday's (1973, 1985, 1993) seven language functions.

Engage students in instructional conversations that are thought-provoking

- Design and deliver activities that require students to engage in goal-driven academic conversations.
- Listen carefully to assess and assist student understanding, and question students on their views, judgments, and/or rationales.
- Ensure a high rate of student interaction.

> **Use visual organizers to support thinking to learn**
>
> - Use organizers systematically to support specific types of thinking consistently.
> - Provide direct, explicit instruction for using visual organizers to think to learn.
> - Engage others in the school and district in use of the same organizers to allow for consistent thinking to learn among the student population.

SUMMARY

In this chapter, we discussed the last prong of the four-pronged framework: learning as a cognitive process. We described thinking to learn as an active, socially constructed process (Vygotsky, 1978) that requires negotiating meaning (Long, 1983). We discussed how learning is dependent on our prior knowledge and depth of familiarity and membership in our learning community to understand a learning task and complete it successfully. We explored Halliday's (1973, 1985, 1993) language functions as they apply to learning contexts. Drawing from Bloom, we investigated how to apply these functions with thinking-to-learn tasks.

Our next chapter will present the importance of family engagement in student learning.

REFERENCES

Anderson, L. W., & Krathwohl, D. R. (Eds.). (2001). *A taxonomy for learning, teaching, and assessing: A revision of Bloom's Taxonomy of Educational Objectives.* New York, NY: Longman.

Bloom, B. S. (1956). *Taxonomy of educational objectives, Book 1: Cognitive domain.* New York, NY: Longman.

Feuerstein, R., Feuerstein, R. S., & Falik, L. H. (2010). *Beyond smarter: Mediated learning and the brain's capacity for change.* New York, NY: Teachers College Press.

Gee, J. P. (1990). *Social linguistics and literacies: Ideology in discourses.* London, England: Falmer Press.

Halliday, M. A. K. (1973). *Explorations in the functions of language.* London: Edward Arnold.

Halliday, M. A. K. (1985). *Spoken and written language.* Oxford, England: Oxford University Press.

Halliday, M. A. K. (1993). Towards a language-based theory of learning. *Linguistics and Education, 5,* 93–116.

Hyerle, D. (2004). Thinking maps as a transformational language for learning. In D. Hyerle (Ed.), *Student success with thinking maps: School-based research, results, and models for achievement using visual tools.* Thousand Oaks, CA: Corwin.

Jensen, E. J. (2005). *Teaching with the brain in mind* (2nd ed.). Alexandria, VA: Association for Supervision and Curriculum Development.

Long, M. H. (1983). Linguistic and conversational adjustments to nonnative speakers. *Journal of Studies in Second Language Acquisition, 5,* 177–193.

Peregoy, S. E., & Boyle, O. F. (2008). Reading, writing and learning in ESL: A resource book for teaching K–12 English learners (5th ed.). Boston, MA: Allyn & Bacon.

Rogoff, B. (1990). *Apprenticeship in thinking: Cognitive development in social context.* New York, NY: Oxford University Press.

Vygotsky, L. S. (1978). *Mind in society: The development of higher psychological processes* (M. Cole, V. John-Steiner, S. Scribner, & E. Souberman, Ed. & Trans.). Cambridge, MA: Harvard University Press.

Wells, G. (1994). The complementary contributions of Halliday and Vygotsky to a "language-based theory of learning." *Linguistics and Education, 6,* 41–90.

Zwiers, J. (2007). *Building academic language: Essential practices for content classrooms.* San Francisco, CA: Jossey-Bass.

Zwiers, J. (2012). *Talk is priceless: Building students' skills for powerful academic conversations.* Paper presented at the annual conference of the Massachusetts Teachers of Speakers of Other Languages, Framingham, MA.

ENDNOTE

1. Gee (1990) refers to discourse as "a socially accepted association among ways of using language, of thinking, feeling, believing, valuing, and acting that can be used to identify oneself as a member of the socially accepted group" (p. 143).

7 Engaging in Parent Partnerships

Why are school–parent partnerships essential for student learning?

Many of us want to build strong parent partnerships and are not sure how this can best be accomplished. Let's visit Mr. Ortega's classroom as he readies for a parent conference, one of the typical events that occur in schools across our nation.

Mr. Ortega teaches sixth-grade English at an urban middle school in the Midwest. Most of the middle school's parents,[1] like many throughout the United States, work and are unable to attend parent conference meetings during the school day. In response, Mr. Ortega and his team of colleagues schedule parent conferences directly before school, after school, and in the early evening to make them more accessible. They have been using this flexible scheduling plan for the past 5 years and found it to be a better means for parent participation.

Each member of Mr. Ortega's team of teachers, representing math, science, social studies, and English, is assigned a group of 30 students and is the point of contact for the parents of these students. Mr. Ortega and his teammates generally collect notes and information from each other as well as their team's special education, ESL, and other staff about their group of students so that they can prepare for parent conferences. The teachers also frequently try to phone parents when their children are doing well and when they are not, and they try their best to be available for parents.

The parent conference is one of the routine events that occur for parents. During the fall term, the school has an Open House, parent conferences, and a potluck supper; during the spring term, there are parent conferences and a class play that the sixth graders perform. On occasion, parents are asked to volunteer for specific tasks such as fund-raising events. Less than a quarter of the parent population participates in the Open House and parent conference events, and only a handful in the other activities. If we were to visit the middle school, we would rarely see the presence of parents other than the ones who are picking their child up from school or coming in because their child is having problems. While staff would like more parent involvement, they do not want to assume that it is not occurring because this is a norm for parents of middle school–aged students and are seeking ways for more involvement.

The following reflection prompts have been separated for individual study and team study. Complete the prompt that applies to your particular context.

REFLECTION PROMPT FOR INDIVIDUAL STUDY

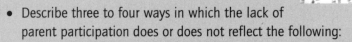

Time for Reflection:

Reflect on the following question, and write a response.

- Describe three to four ways in which the lack of parent participation does or does not reflect the following:

  o your parents' experience with middle school conferences

  o your experience conducting parent conferences

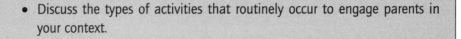

REFLECTION PROMPT FOR TEAM STUDY AND OUR-O-LOGUE

Time for Reflection:

Reflect on the following question, write a response, and prepare to discuss it with your team.

- Discuss the types of activities that routinely occur to engage parents in your context.

Let's take a quick peek at the parent conference that Mr. Ortega holds with Mr. and Mrs. Brown, the parents of his student Sofia. Mr. Ortega has prepared for the conference by gathering information from his colleagues about how Sofia is doing in their classes and has some samples of her work. He invites the Browns to join him at a round table to create a comfortable seating arrangement for the conference, which begins with Mr. Ortega describing Sofia's progress in her academic classes. When the Browns ask questions about her progress in the classes that he does not teach, he refers to his notes and tries his best to respond in a kind manner. The exchange is generally one in which Mr. Ortega controls most of the talk and conducts it in a report mode about Sofia's academic progress. After about 20 minutes, he asks the Browns if they have any questions. They want to know that Sofia is progressing in her classes and is a well-behaved student. After Mr. Ortega provides this assurance, the conference concludes—just in time for Mr. Ortega to meet with the next set of parents.

THE COMPLEX RELATIONSHIPS BETWEEN SCHOOLS AND FAMILIES

The importance of family–school engagement[2] is well documented (Bartel-Haring & Younkin, 2012; Delpit, 1995; Epstein, 1986; Henderson,

Mapp, Johnson, & Davies, 2007; Lawrence-Lightfoot, 2003; Yoshikawa, 2011). Without question, the literature refers to it as a critical element of a child's education. It is not a hidden dimension. Many parents are conditioned to be involved in their child's school in one way or another, and teachers are conditioned to work with parents. Indeed, the terms *parent–school partnerships* and *family–school engagement* are not foreign to most educators, parents, and the American public at large. At the time of this writing, for example, a simple Google search of the term *parent–school partnerships* yielded 12,700,000 results, and *family–school engagement* 491,000,000!

From the moment a child leaves his or her family to enter an early education and care setting, educators and parents become involved with one another, and this relationship continues, to some degree or other, throughout a child's education (Henderson et al., 2007; Lawrence-Lightfoot, 2003).

The following reflection prompts have been separated for individual study and team study. Complete the prompt that applies to your particular context.

REFLECTION PROMPT FOR INDIVIDUAL STUDY

Time for Reflection:

Reflect on the following question, and write a response.

- Describe the ways in which the parent conference scenario between Mr. Ortega and Mr. and Mrs. Brown does or does not reflect your experience attending or conducting parent conferences.

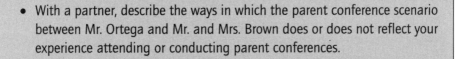

REFLECTION PROMPT FOR TEAM STUDY AND OUR-O-LOGUE

Time for Reflection:

Reflect on the following question, write a response, and prepare to discuss it with your team.

- With a partner, describe the ways in which the parent conference scenario between Mr. Ortega and Mr. and Mrs. Brown does or does not reflect your experience attending or conducting parent conferences.

While establishing relationships with families is an important goal, it is not easy to do for many reasons. One is that many teacher preparation programs do not offer much training in this critical area (Lawrence-Lightfoot, 2003). A second reason is that the spaces for these relationships, such as the parent–teacher conferences and Open House events at Mr. Ortega's middle school, are not conducive to creating close relationships due to their routinized and formal nature. A third reason is that some teachers do not expect, and rarely ask for, parental involvement (Epstein, 1986). Additionally, parents may represent different cultural experiences (including economic, racial, linguistic, and more), and teachers may find it challenging to build relationships with families whose experiences are different from their own. Moreover, establishing relationships with parents takes careful planning and time. However, as we will see in this chapter, family engagement is worth the investment.

APPLICATION OF OUR FOUR-PRONGED FRAMEWORK

Up until this point in the book, we have not discussed family engagement explicitly. Our focus has been on creating high-quality learning environments using a four-pronged framework for understanding and applying learning as a sociocultural, literacy, academic, and cognitive process with students. In this chapter, we will apply the four prongs to family engagement, and we will begin by discussing the complexities and fragilities of the relationships between parents and their child's school.

INTERCONNECTEDNESS OF TWO SYSTEMS

School and parent systems greatly influence a child's development (Bartel-Haring & Younkin, 2012). This might seem like an obvious statement because so much of a child's waking hours are spent either at home or in school. However, it is the interconnectedness between these two that is of importance. While we might not think of this in terms of how one affects the other, developmental theorists Bronfenbrenner and Ceci (1994) hypothesize that the unique ways in which the two systems interact has a great influence on a child's development and genetic potential. They use the term *bioecological* in reference to this phenomenon. Bartel-Haring and Younkin (2012) refer to this interactive environmental phenomenon as one "spilling over" into the other and vice versa. It should not be surprising to read this from our own unique personal perspectives. Our families influence our development. Our schools influence our development. The interconnectedness between the two environments has an impact on our development—as does our genetic potential or what we might refer to as *nurture plus nature.*

It is important to consider the ways in which we build connections with families. This is especially true when these relationships cross over such important demographic differences as culture, ethnicity, income, education, and age, among other variables. For example, suppose a parent does not believe that it is his or her place to be involved with his or her child's school. While we might believe in the value of parent–school partnerships, the ways that we establish these relationships may not be in sync with parents' value systems or beliefs. An important overriding and perhaps overlooked element to consider is how well we understand and complement parents' personal, social, cultural, and world experiences and create opportunities that match and are empathetic to this sociocultural dimension.

SOCIOCULTURAL INFLUENCES ON OUR BELIEFS

Factors related to diversity have been found to affect our beliefs about students and their families and may not present us in the most positive light. According to Hollins and Guzman (2005), most of the nation's teachers and teacher educators are "White middle class monolingual English speaking with limited experience with people and cultures other than their own" (p. 485). Further, they are not prepared to work with students who come from cultures other than their own and prefer working with students whose experiences are similar to theirs (Hollins & Guzman, 2005).

What makes this a particularly challenging finding is that academic language learners do not represent the same cultural group as do the majority of their teachers. As educators, we carry and generally covet academic language. We engage in a lot of academic language behaviors at work and home. The limits of our experience with and professional training about academic language learners present us with complex productive tensions, especially when it comes to building effective parent partnerships. How can we transform our current practices so that we create more positive relationships and engagement with our students and their families?

The following reflection prompts have been separated for individual study and team study. Complete the prompt that applies to your particular context.

REFLECTION PROMPT FOR INDIVIDUAL STUDY

Time for Reflection:

Reflect on the following question, and write a response.

- Think about Mr. Ortega's middle school. Describe two to three activities that you think Mr. Ortega and his team could do to increase the level of parent involvement. What would be your goals and objectives for these activities?

**REFLECTION PROMPT FOR TEAM
STUDY AND OUR-O-LOGUE**

Time for Reflection:

Reflect on the following question, write a response,
and prepare to discuss it with your team.

- Mr. Ortega and his colleagues do not experience a high level of parent
  participation, particularly among specific groups of parents. Consider your
  particular context with a partner. What activities can you do to enhance
  parent involvement/engagement?

Let's look at three different students in Mr. Ortega's class so that we have a context from which to build our discussion about parent engagement. Lara Pacheco is a U.S. citizen, but her parents are undocumented immigrants who have lived in the United States for well over a decade. They speak English well, work many hours per week (sometimes double shifts when they can), and care deeply about Lara. Like many parents of the country's 5.5 million citizen children of undocumented immigrants (Yoshikawa, 2011), her parents live in constant fear of deportation as well as losing their jobs and home. They are also afraid to sign any legal document, including what is needed for checking and savings accounts. In addition, they are afraid to complete any of the documents that would have been made available to Lara, including the benefits she is entitled to receive. This includes, according to Yoshikawa (2011), the school's breakfast and lunch programs, health care, and other important benefits that U.S. citizen parents can and do obtain. While Lara's parents would like to be involved in her education, their level of chronic stress is an overriding factor impeding their limited participation in her education.

James Wilson is another of Mr. Ortega's students. He lives with his father, who dropped out of high school in the 10th grade and has many bad memories of school. While he wants James to do well in school, he does not feel comfortable coming to the school.

Sofia Brown is a third student of Mr. Ortega's. Her parents, whom we met earlier, come to every conference, frequently email Mr. Ortega with questions about Sofia or her English class, and want to be as involved as they possibly can.

So Mr. Ortega has at least three students with widely differing home experiences. It's likely that each of the 30 students' parents has unique personal beliefs, cultures, and expectations for their child's education.

WHAT CAN WE LEARN FROM THE RESEARCH?

Despite the differences among Mr. Ortega's students, models of high levels of collaboration between schools and parents can be highly beneficial, especially when we take time to think seriously about what is needed to transform our schools so that they have effective and sustained partnerships with parents. Joyce Epstein (1986), a highly regarded sociologist on parent–school engagement practices, has studied parents' perceptions of teachers. Before launching into the findings of this important study, Epstein provides us with information on teachers' attitudes about parent involvement. For ease of discussion, these are depicted in Figure 7.1 and reflect a range of beliefs.

Figure 7.1 Teachers' Diverse Perceptions of Parent Involvement

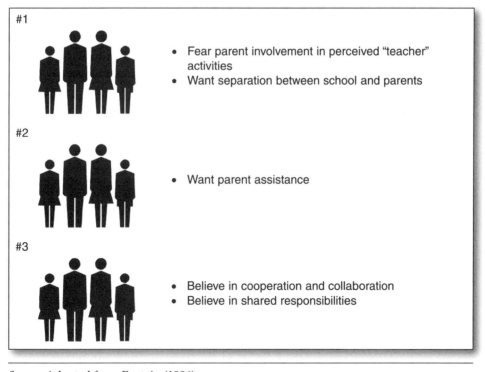

#1
- Fear parent involvement in perceived "teacher" activities
- Want separation between school and parents

#2
- Want parent assistance

#3
- Believe in cooperation and collaboration
- Believe in shared responsibilities

Source: Adapted from Epstein (1986).

According to Epstein (1986), we enact what we believe. Thus, the first group in Figure 7.1 is less likely to enact powerful family engagement environments than is the last. While this is important to consider, equally relevant are parents' perceptions about their child's school and teachers. Let's look at the population of parents that were studied.

Parents of 1,269 students representing 82 first-, third-, and fifth-grade classrooms in Maryland were asked to respond to a questionnaire, and 59% of them responded. The responses were analyzed for demographic variables, parents' attitude toward their child's school, parents' level of involvement and communication in school, and their reactions to programs and practices of teachers. Ninety-two percent of respondents were female, 62% were White, and 36% were Black, and there was a broad range of levels of education. Figure 7.2 depicts this range.

Figure 7.3 provides us with information about parents' perceptions of their child's school. While parents' range of educational experiences is important to note, we can learn a lot from their perceptions of their child's school as well as their beliefs about what is needed.

The majority of respondents, across all levels of education, reported that they were involved with their child's education. They read to their child or their child read to them, they discussed school with their child,

Figure 7.2 Level of Parent Education

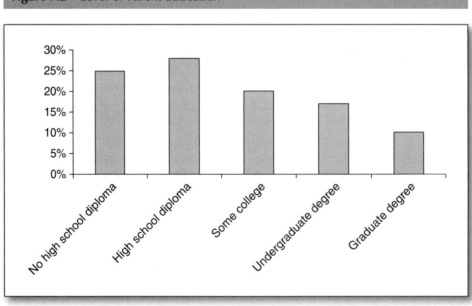

Source: Adapted from Epstein (1986).

Figure 7.3 Parents' Perceptions

Areas that were positive:

- The school and teachers were looked on favorably.
- The school was well run.
- Goals were compatible with theirs.

Areas needing strengthening:

- Teachers could do more to involve parents.
- School–parent communication was too informational.
- The school and teachers provided limited encouragement for communication.
- Parents are rarely involved in school activities.
- Parents of older children did not feel as confident in supporting older children as they did younger children in school.
- Teachers could do more to show parents how to help their child with school-work at home.

Source: Adapted from Epstein (1986).

they played interactive games, and they supervised their child doing school-based activities. All of these activities do indeed support a child's education. In addition, the vast majority (90%) indicated that their attitudes about their child's school and teachers were positive. Parents reported feeling that their child's school was "well run," that "they felt comfortable," and that "they and the teachers had the same goals for their child" (Epstein, 1986, p. 280). These are encouraging findings. First, parents support their child's schooling at home, and second, they feel positive about their child's school.

At the same time, most of the parents stated that their child's teachers could strengthen their level of parental involvement. They were referring to a specific type of involvement that they believed would be helpful. Parents stated that communication that they received from the school and their child's teacher mostly came in the form of routine and impersonal information such as schedules, report cards, and emergency procedures. There was little personal relational communication between the teacher and parents about their child. A second finding was also significant as it reflected the amount of time that parents participated in their child's school. Only 4% were actively involved on a regular basis.

The following reflection prompts have been separated for individual study and team study. Complete the prompt that applies to your particular context.

REFLECTION PROMPT FOR INDIVIDUAL STUDY

Time for Reflection:

Reflect on the following question, and write a response.

- Think carefully about Epstein's (1986) findings as they relate to your particular context. Design an activity for strengthening one or two of the bulleted areas from the second list in Figure 7.3.

REFLECTION PROMPT FOR TEAM STUDY AND OUR-O-LOGUE

Time for Reflection

Reflect on the following question, write an answer, and prepare to discuss it with your team.

- Discuss how Epstein's (1986) findings do or do not reflect your particular context. Whether there is a high or low level of parent involvement in your context, discuss two to three activities that you can do to strengthen it meaningfully.

Let's look at these findings a little more closely by using our four-pronged framework.

LEARNING IS A SOCIOCULTURAL PROCESS

In Chapter 3, we discussed the importance of building relationships with students and making engaging connections with their learning. We also discussed the importance of pair and small-group work as a means for students to learn effectively with and from each other. These ideas complement the collectivist cultures of many of our students and their families. Drawing from Hofstede (2001; Hofstede & Hofstede, 2005), DeCapua and Marshall (2010), and Zacarian and Haynes (2012), we learned that students from collectivist cultures favor group harmony and the good of the group over individualism. These same cultural beliefs and ideologies apply to many parents and complement one of the primary findings of Epstein's (1986) research: Parents want to build a personal relationship with their child's teacher.

Following the sociocultural frame, we need to look closely at the routine events and activities that typically occur in school and flow from school to home. We must ask ourselves how they complement the cultural beliefs of many parents and the findings of Epstein's (1986) study. We are likely to find that much of what we do is counter to what is needed. Open House, for example, is a ritualized event that commonly occurs in American schools (Zacarian, 2007a, 2011). At the secondary level, most parents know that they and the entire parent community will follow an abbreviated schedule of their child's school day and that Open House does not include a time for asking personal questions about their child. The following exchange between two parents is typical of this ritualized event. One parent is familiar with the event and the second, though not as familiar, knows what to ask about it so that he too may become familiar with it.

Figure 7.4   Parent Exchange at an Open House

Parent 1:   So what do we do now?

Parent 2:   You'll get Janet's Monday class schedule. The bell will ring, you'll hear Mr. Martin, the principal, announce that we'll go to our kids' first period class. It'll last about 10 minutes. The bell will ring again, and we'll go to our kids' second class. If Janet has a study hall, you can go to the cafeteria for cookies and coffee and to learn about the Parent Council. Definitely stop there; the cookies are usually good!

Source: Zacarian (2011, p. 115).

The quick exchange is packed with implied meanings about a culture in which most of us have been conditioned. The second parent learns very quickly about the event and rules for behaving in it. It's likely that he has also participated in events such as this since his child was in kindergarten. Another routine event is the parent conference. This, too, is loaded with implied rules for acting and behaving (Lawrence-Lightfoot, 2003) and is not exactly a setting in which relationships are built. Rather, it is one that Lawrence-Lightfoot (2003) aptly claims involves a powerful imbalance of authority in terms of a teacher's role over a parent's child.

Because this meeting also is so ritualized, most parents have been conditioned to ask questions about their child in response to a teacher's report of the child's performance and behavior. While this might not be the case all of the time, the example of Mr. Ortega's parent conference with Mr. and Mrs. Brown illustrates a typical example of what occurs across our nation.

Thus, these two commonly occurring ritualized events, Open House and parent conferences, do not offer much in the way of matching or complementing the sociocultural frame that centers on building relationships; an understanding of parents' personal, cultural, and world knowledge; and a high level of interactions. What can be done? A lot!

One of the key findings and suggestions of Epstein (1986, 2001) and other experts on parent engagement (e.g., Christenson & Sheridan, 2001; Espinosa, 2010; Henderson et al., 2007) is that we must establish meaningful and powerful communications between home and school as this greatly benefits students' academic and social success. Building these into our practice should be a priority. There are many strategies for complementing the sociocultural frame with families using an asset-based model of family engagement. This model calls for a primary belief and commitment among teachers and administrators that parents are rich and welcome resources and contributors to their child's education.

Enrollment practices are an important first consideration. Whether districts have a centralized or local process, it usually includes the steps listed in Figure 7.5.

The process, like Epstein's (1986) findings, is heavily loaded with information giving and receiving that has little to do with creating a welcoming environment. Gathering collaborative teams together to create a process for welcoming parents is an important must-do. An example of this is a new initiative that Mr. Ortega's middle school has recently implemented. A team of teachers, including general classroom, special education, ESL, and specialists, as well as a guidance counselor, an outreach worker, and the school principal have collaborated to make the process of enrollment more welcoming. The new process involves students and parents assisting in orientation activities. To implement the new plan, letters were sent to parents seeking volunteers for this work, and school staff recruited student

Figure 7.5 Enrollment Process

Step 1. Parents generally bring

- Immunization forms
- Child's prior school transcripts
- Birth certificate
- Proof of residency

Step 2. Parents generally complete

- Home language survey
- Emergency information
- Prior transcript release form

Step 3. Parents typically must understand Steps 1 and 2 as well as

- Prior transcript review process
- Daily schedule, school calendar
- Course information
- Immunization process
- Emergency procedures
- Students' rights and code of conduct
- Process for applying for free or reduced lunch program
- Extracurricular activities

Source: Zacarian & Haynes (2012).

volunteers. Within a few weeks, teams of parents and students joined the effort, brainstormed ideas, and implemented a plan for welcoming families. Included in the plan is a "shadow" peer for new students during the first few days of school and a team of parent volunteers who reach out to families that are new to the community. Also, knowing that some of the newcomers are children of undocumented parents, school guidance and adjustment counselors and outreach workers meet regularly with community organizations. They have developed ways for providing families with what Yoshikawa (2011) calls *trusted support* in obtaining public services.

Another example of supporting personal family engagement is the arts. Events including music, dance, plays, and other performance modes that complement parent communities are a fine way of capturing parent interest in their child's school (Henderson et al., 2007). Rather than wait for the first month of school to pass and parent conferences to commence, these types of welcoming activities bring parents to their child's school for the sole and important purpose of relationship and social building. Parents can also be a fine resource for this type of activity. Activities such as these social ones help provide a welcoming and inclusive social atmosphere for parents. A good rule of thumb is to create two to three social activities to precede an academic activity such as Open House or parent conferences. They help support families and schools in working collaboratively and can help schools move away from a formal, impersonal model to a more personal and relational one.

The following reflection prompts have been separated for individual study and team study. Complete the prompt that applies to your particular context.

REFLECTION PROMPT FOR INDIVIDUAL STUDY

Time for Reflection:

Reflect on the following question, and write a response.

- Drawing from the sociocultural frame, describe two to three activities that you would do to build relationships. Select from, and expand on, one or more of the choices below:

  o Work with a collaborative team of teachers, parents, and students.

  o Develop a plan for developing parent partnerships in your classroom.

o Determine changes that could be made to improve accessibility for families and students.

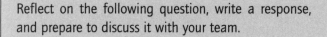

REFLECTION PROMPT FOR TEAM STUDY AND OUR-O-LOGUE

Time for Reflection:

Reflect on the following question, write a response, and prepare to discuss it with your team.

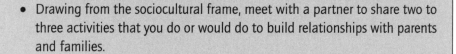

- Drawing from the sociocultural frame, meet with a partner to share two to three activities that you do or would do to build relationships with parents and families.

LEARNING ACADEMIC LANGUAGE TO BUILD LITERACY

Many teachers and administrators are becoming more and more familiar with the rich assets that parents can and do provide to student learning. They see benefits from a variety of perspectives, not the least of which are the rich practice opportunities for students to learn outside of school. A fine example of this, related to language and literacy learning, is a project-based learning unit by the National Writing Project (2012). Pairs and small groups of students conducted interviews of a family member or friend about his or her immigrant experience. Students then collected these stories and produced a digital storytelling film. It placed parents at the center of the project. Parents and friends who were the interview subjects, as well as other family members, came to the culminating activity of viewing the film. The power of this project can be underscored from a variety of perspectives, not the least of which is parent engagement.

There are countless ways to involve families in student learning. Helping parents learn about what is occurring in school is key for promoting this type of parent understanding.

The following reflection prompts have been separated for individual study and team study. Complete the prompt that applies to your particular context.

REFLECTION PROMPT FOR INDIVIDUAL STUDY

Time for Reflection:

Reflect on the following question, and write a response.

- Describe two to three activities that you would do to increase parent engagement in a subject that you teach. How will these activities draw from the assets and resources of parents?

REFLECTION PROMPT FOR TEAM STUDY AND OUR-O-LOGUE

Time for Reflection:

Reflect on the following question, write a response, and prepare to discuss it with your team.

- Create an activity that engages parents in an academic area that you teach. Be creative.

LEARNING IS ACADEMIC

Much of what we do as effective educators is build learning from our students' backgrounds (Jensen, 1998; Tovani, 2000). Building connections is more than an academic process. It is made more meaningful when it is connected to our students' personal, cultural, language, and world experiences as well as their prior academic knowledge (Haynes & Zacarian, 2010; Zacarian, 2011). Building learning experiences from students' background knowledge should point us to making connections with families. Families are phenomenal resources and can be powerful partners in the learning process when we take time to connect learning with their lives (Moll, 1992). Further, as we saw from Epstein's (1986) findings, parents are eager to learn about their child's learning. Henderson et al. (2007) affirm Epstein's findings and provide us with many ideas for engaging families in their child's learning process; they suggest events such as "reading workshop, family math night, home learning packets, parent-run study centers, and career portfolio nights" (p. 82) as key supports in this collaborative school–family engagement process.

An important consideration for connecting academic learning with families is that we need to organize these events so that they are in sync with social and academic activities that occur during the school year. An Open House is simply not enough. A key means for supporting families is to make the learning goals for students explicit and visible. Displaying student work, sharing student portfolios, sending home information about the overarching goals and objectives of curriculum being studied, inviting families into the classroom to see learning in action, creating curriculum newsletters, and holding family events that center on student learning are all ways to connect families to their child's learning.

The following reflection prompts have been separated for individual study and team study. Complete the prompt that applies to your particular context.

REFLECTION PROMPT FOR INDIVIDUAL STUDY

Time for Reflection:

Reflect on the following question, and write a response.

- Think carefully about Epstein's (1986) findings about parent involvement. What are some of the key reasons you believe that the parents in this study were not actively involved in their child's school? What leads you to think in this way?

**REFLECTION PROMPT FOR TEAM
STUDY AND OUR-O-LOGUE**

Time for Reflection:

Reflect on the following question, write a response,
and prepare to discuss it with your team.

- Think carefully about Epstein's (1986) findings about parent involvement. Create an activity that will support your students' academic literacy development that draws from parents as rich and valuable
  resources.

LEARNING IS A COGNITIVE PROCESS

Children spend many more hours out of school than they do in school.
Much can be done during this time to support the acquisition of thinking-
to-learn skills. The first is to create opportunities for students to engage
with their families in this important process. To explain how this works,
let's look at two examples. In the first, Mrs. Melkin, a third-grade teacher,
provides a range of home-based assignments to help her students
become more adept at using the language functions that were presented in
Chapter 6 (Halliday, 1985). In the second example, Mrs. Lee, a high school
English teacher, wants to build her student's analytic and evaluative skills.
Mrs. Melkin and Mrs. Lee's states have adopted the Common Core State
Standards (2010), in which "presentation of knowledge and ideas" is an
important element.

Making Thinking Skills Explicit for Parents to Support

An important feature of Mrs. Melkin's third grade-class is her capacity to make learning explicit. She helps her students learn how to ask questions and work in pairs and groups (she assigns various roles for speakers and listeners). She is currently working on her students' capacity to express their feelings and emotions in a written format through information gathering. Drawing from the writing standards in the Common Core State Standards (2010, p. 20), she wants her students to build their capacity to use imaginative language to describe details, thoughts, and feelings, and temporal words and phrases (e.g., *before, during, after*) to support their use of sequential writing.

Mrs. Melkin's school is located in a poor, densely wooded rural area in New Hampshire. Each year, she gathers a box of small rocks and assigns one rock to each of her students. For this assignment, she asks them to take the rock to an area in the woods near their home, to place it on the ground, and to write about the rock as if it were alive and telling someone about what it is experiencing. She sends her students home with a note describing the writing activity. In the note, she provides parents with the same essential question that she has provided her students: *Why is it important to use our imagination to describe the world around us?* She tells parents that the purpose of the writing activity is to promote their child's creativity to use imaginative language, to sequence a story, and to become more comfortable using descriptive language. She asks them to talk to their child about the rock story. In addition, she provides them with suggested descriptive language and temporal words that their child should use. During the school's Family Night, which occurs during the first month of school, Mrs. Melkin makes sure to greet the families and show them various models of "rock stories" that prior students have written. Her intent is to show parents a variety of writing samples so that they, in turn, will help their children engage in it. She also coordinates the writing project to conclude just before parent conferences so that it provides them with a common topic for discussion. Home activities like this are part of her routine to build family partnerships and support her students' thinking-to-learn skills.

Mrs. Lee is an 11th-grade English teacher in an urban city in the South. In her community, the city's trash haulers were threatening to strike in their effort to be awarded a better contract. She saw this as an important opportunity to explore a social justice environmental issue through a debate format. Drawing from the Common Core State Standards (2010) in the areas of listening and speaking, she planned a unit of study in which her students would "use multiple sources of information, evaluate a speaker's point of view . . . present information with supporting evidence . . . and make strategic use of digital media" (p. 50). She worked with her students to plan interviews of family members, friends, and workers from the waste management company to learn about their thoughts for and against the strike. She also engaged her students in reading legal contracts about whether the trash haulers had the right to strike. She then separated her class into two groups. One was assigned the pro side of the strike, and the other the con side.

Using the information gathered from the interviews they had recorded digitally and contract information about the legal right to strike, each side was asked to prepare and practice their debate with family members and friends. Mrs. Lee also provided families with information about the debate format, her goals for this unity of study, and the criterion that would be used judge the debate. Because this was a hot topic in the community, families took a keen interest in the students' work. A week before the actual class debate occurred, Mrs. Lee required her class to switch sides. Drawing from the Common Core State Standards, she sent a letter home to explain that the purpose of switching was to help students apprentice the type of listening and speaking skills that they needed. The actual debate occurred as a culminating activity in the early evening. Many parents and community members attended the debate. By the time it occurred, Mrs. Lee's students had already had multiple opportunities to practice this type of format. Their thinking-to-learn skills were greatly utilized throughout the unit.

The following reflection prompts have been separated for individual study and team study. Complete the prompt that applies to your particular context.

REFLECTION PROMPT FOR INDIVIDUAL STUDY

Time for Reflection:

Reflect on the following question, and write a response.

- Think carefully about Mrs. Melkin's and Mrs. Lee's application of learning as a cognitive process with families. Describe two to three ways in which you might apply these ideas to your work.

REFLECTION PROMPT FOR TEAM STUDY AND OUR-O-LOGUE

Time for Reflection:

Reflect on the following question, write a response, and prepare to discuss it with your team.

- With a partner, think carefully about Mrs. Melkin's and Mrs. Lee's applications of learning as a cognitive process with families. Create two to three activities that apply these ideas to your particular contexts.

PUTTING THE FOUR-PRONGED FRAMEWORK INTO PRACTICE TO SUPPORT PARENT ENGAGEMENT

Build relationships with parents

- Personally connect with each student's family.
- Empathetically understand each family.
- Infuse this understanding into the learning environment.
- Continuously welcome and promote parent engagement.
- Create socially welcoming gatherings where parents can participate actively.
- Help families see value in learning and their child's future.

Connect curriculum with parents' lives to support learning in and out of school

- Connect learning to parents' lives with multiple socially relevant connections made between home and school.
- Include parents in student learning.

Understand parents' academic language level

- Communicate with parents in a language that is comprehensible.
- Include and integrate home–school activities with academic language learning.

Involve parents and families in their child's academic, curricular learning

- Consistently reach out to parents and families about what is being learned.
- Encourage routine parent participation in learning.
- Connect curriculum and home.
- Include activities for engaging parents in curriculum, including reading workshop, family math nights, parent-run study centers, and college-career nights.

Involve parents and families in supporting their child's thinking-to-learn skills

- Continuously and routinely share the purpose of learning activities with parents.
- Provide parents with continuous explanation of learning objectives and what students will do to learn.
- Hold parent meetings to explain learning goals and activities.
- Incorporate learning activities that can be done at home to support the learning process.
- Hold family events that support thinking-to-learn goals.

SUMMARY

In this chapter, we discussed the importance of family engagement and applied our four-pronged framework to the notion of building collaborative partnerships. We began by talking about the importance of family engagement and the complexities related to enacting it effectively. Included in our discussion was a description of the general teaching and teacher-educator populations and the need to broaden our understanding of student and family populations that are different from our own.

In our discussion of the sociocultural, academic language, academic, and cognitive learning frames, we explored Bartel-Haring and Younkin's (2012) theories of how school and parent systems affect child development. We drew from Bronfenbrenner and Ceci's (1994) theory of bioecology to understand the ways in which the two systems interact. We also highlighted the importance of building strong relationships with families by building connections with their personal, social, cultural, and world experiences.

Epstein's (1986) research about parents' perceptions and attitudes about their child's school and teachers provided us with important information to consider when developing parent partnerships. Drawing from her study, several examples can help us create schools that build strong school–family partnerships and relationships that are intentionally focused to support academic language learning, subject matter development, and thinking-to-learn skills.

Home–school engagement is a key contributor to student success and membership in the school community. When the ideas and strategies from this chapter are applied in classroom, school, and home environments, families and students can greatly benefit.

In our next chapter, we will discuss the importance of making data-driven decisions.

REFERENCES

Bartel-Haring, S., & Younkin, F. L. (2012). Family distance regulation and school engagement in middle-school-aged children. *Family Relations Interdisciplinary Journal of Applied Family Studies, 61,* 192–206.

Bronfenbrenner, U., & Ceci, S. (1994). Nature-nurture reconceptualized in developmental perspective: A bioecological model. *Psychological Review, 101,* 568–586.

Christenson, S. L., & Sheridan, S. M. (2001). *School and families: Creating essential connections for learning.* New York, NY: Guilford Press.

Common Core State Standards Initiative. (2010). *Common Core State Standards for English language arts and literacy in history/social studies, science, and technical subjects.* Retrieved from http://www.corestandards.org/assets/CCSSI_ELA%20Standards.pdf

DeCapua, A., & Marshall, H. (2010). Serving ELLs with limited or interrupted education: Intervention that works. *TESOL Journal, 1,* 49–70. Retrieved from http://www.tesolmedia.com/docs/TJ/firstissue/06_TJ_DeCapuaMarshall.pdf

Delpit, L. (1995). *Other people's children: Cultural conflict in the classroom.* New York, NY: New Press.

Epstein, J. L. (1986). Parents' reactions to teacher practices of parent involvement. *Elementary School Journal, 86,* 277–294.

Epstein, J. L. (2001). *School, family, and community partnerships: Preparing educators for improving schools.* Boulder, CO: Westview Press.

Espinosa, L. (2010). *Getting it right for young children with diverse backgrounds: Applying research to improve practice.* Upper Saddle River, NJ: Pearson.

Halliday, M. A. K. (1985). *Spoken and written language.* Oxford, England: Oxford University Press.

Haynes, J., & Zacarian, D. (2010). *Teaching English language learners across the content areas.* Alexandria, VA: Association for Supervision and Curriculum Development.

Henderson, A. T., Mapp, K. L. Johnson, V. R., & Davies, D. (2007). Beyond the bake sale: The essential guide to family-school partnerships. New York, NY: New Press.

Hofstede, G. (2001). *Culture's consequences: Comparing values, behaviors, institutions, and organizations across nations* (2nd ed.). Thousand Oaks, CA: Sage.

Hofstede, G., & Hofstede, G. J. (2005). *Cultures and organizations: Software of the mind* (2nd ed.). New York, NY: McGraw-Hill.

Hollins, E., & Guzman, M. T. (2005). Research on preparing teachers for diverse populations. In M. Cochran & K. M. Zeichner (Eds.), *Studying teacher education: The report of the AERA Panel on Research and Teacher Education* (pp. 477–548). Mahwah, NJ: Lawrence Erlbaum.

Jensen, E. (1998). *Teaching with the brain in mind.* Alexandria, VA: Association for Supervision and Curriculum Development.

Lawrence-Lightfoot, S. (2003). *The essential conversation: What parents and teachers can learn from each other.* New York, NY: Random House.

Moll, L. (1992). Bilingual classroom studies and community analysis: Some recent trends. *Educational Researcher, 21,* 20–24.

National Writing Project. (2012). *Literacy, ELL, and digital storytelling: 21st century learning in action.* Retrieved from http://www.nwp.org/cs/public/print/resource/2790

Tovani, C. (2000). *I read it, but I don't get it: Comprehension strategies for adolescent readers.* Portland, ME: Stenhouse.

Yoshikawa, H. (2011). *Immigrants raising citizens: Undocumented parents and their young children.* New York, NY: Russell Sage Foundation.

Zacarian, D. (2007a). I can't go to college! *Essential Teacher, 4*(4), 10–11.

Zacarian, D. (2007b). Mascot or member. *Essential Teacher, 4*(3), 10–11.

Zacarian, D. (2011). *Transforming schools for English learners: A comprehensive framework for school leaders.* Thousand Oaks, CA: Corwin.

Zacarian, D., & Haynes, J. (2012). *The essential guide for educating beginning English learners.* Thousand Oaks, CA: Corwin.

ENDNOTES

1. *Parent* is used in reference to parents, grandparents, guardians, siblings, and others who have the primary responsibility of caring for a child.

2. The terms *family-school engagement* and *family engagement* are used here to refer to schools that involve families as an integral partner in their students' learning.

8 Making Data-Driven Decisions

> How can we use the four-pronged framework to analyze and strengthen classroom, school, and parent engagement environments?
>
> We begin our discussion by visiting four different locations in the United States and learning how the educators in each place typically evaluate student performance.

Jacob is a freshman in an urban district in Massachusetts. Olivia and Maria are elementary school students, one in a rural community in South Carolina and the other in a large suburban community in Ohio. Bo is an eighth-grade student in a large urban high school in California. Each of their teachers and principals wants them and all of their students to have as solid and academic a program as possible and seeks ways to measure whether their programming is working and how to strengthen areas in need of improvement. They use two primary means for determining success: student attendance as well as student performance on state assessments.

COMMON MEANS FOR DETERMINING STUDENT PERFORMANCE

Attendance

The four students' teachers and principals know that school attendance is critical. Their work operates on the premise that students will attend school every day throughout the academic year. The number of school days and amount of time that students spend learning specific subject matter is based on the standard that students will not miss too much school (Balfanz & Byrnes, 2012). Indeed, each of their schools has policies about absenteeism. Looking at this more carefully, however, they also know that chronic absenteeism is a national epidemic, especially among the nation's poor, and that this is a factor that they must consider carefully for three primary reasons:

- Students who cannot attend due to illness, family responsibilities, housing instability, and the need to work, or involvement in the juvenile justice system
- Students who will not attend to avoid bullying, safety conditions, harassment, and embarrassment
- Students who do not attend because they, or their parents, do not see value in being there (Balfanz & Byrnes, 2012, pp. 4–5)

Unfortunately, many of us do not know why our students miss school (Balfanz & Byrnes, 2012). Rather, the data that we typically collect is about the percentage of students who are attending school (e.g., 80% attend on Monday, 72% on Tuesday) as opposed to the actual students who represent these absences. Further, especially at the secondary level, there are students who attend some but not all of their classes. Learning more about the specifics of this challenge can greatly help us determine an effective and appropriate remedy. One of the primary reasons this is important to our study is that a major reason for chronic absenteeism is that students and their parents do not see value in education (Balfanz & Byrnes, 2012). Our four-pronged framework is intended to remedy this challenge.

Performance on High-Stakes Tests

Jacob, Olivia, Maria, and Bo's teachers and school leaders also know all too well the importance of high-stakes tests. They know that the No Child Left Behind Act (NCLB), the 2001 reauthorization of the Elementary and Secondary Education Act, requires that they create improvement plans that are typically based on the results of their state and local assessments. Analyzing the testing results and creating improvement plans for the students who perform poorly are not easy tasks.

The following reflection prompts have been separated for individual study and team study. Complete the prompt that applies to your particular context.

REFLECTION PROMPT FOR INDIVIDUAL STUDY

Time for Reflection:

Reflect on the following question, and write a response.

- Why do you think analyzing student performance is not an easy task? Discuss two to three challenges that you have experienced or think would occur, and describe some responses that you think might help to remedy these challenges.

REFLECTION PROMPT FOR TEAM STUDY AND OUR-O-LOGUE

Time for Reflection:

Reflect on the following questions, write responses, and prepare to discuss them with your team.

- Do an Internet search of your state's assessment system regarding the grade spans that most apply to your context. Read the information carefully. Do you find it to be easily written and informative? Why or why not?

(Continued)

(Continued)

> • With a partner, discuss two to three strategies that you use or would use to understand or analyze student performance on state measures.

Challenges of Using State Assessment Data to Determine Improvement Measures

Using state assessment data for this purpose can be quite challenging for a number of reasons, not the least of which is the sheer number of students who need analyzing, especially in many large districts. While state systems generate reports on how a whole group does (by state, district, and school) and, under the requirements of NCLB, divide performance results into specific subgroup categories of students as well as individual and parent reports of student progress (U.S. Department of Education, 2007), they generally do so with a broad brush. Some of us also take time to disaggregate this data even further so that we may learn more detailed information about student responses to specific questions and groups within subgroups (e.g., Mexican American and Dominican American students within a Latino subgroup).

Whatever means is used to conduct and complete the analysis, our intent is to arm others and ourselves with information and plans for addressing who needs to improve, what needs to improve, and how improvement goals will be met. For a number of reasons, this is a complex task. Very few of us have been trained to analyze data (Elmore, 2002; Wayman, Midgley, & Stringfield, 2006). Rather, it is expected that, as educators, we have the depth of knowledge and the time that we need to address the underperformance issues that we identify (Wayman et al., 2006). In addition, we often address underperformance by analyzing what students are not doing as opposed to what they are, and we build programming based on this analysis (Love, Stiles, Mudry, & DiRanna, 2008). Moreover, it is expected that the data we receive from state assessments provide us with just what we need to make data-informed decisions about our students. In reality, the results of student performance on state exams are not known for many months after students take the exams. Therefore, we analyze outdated data. To exacerbate this problem further, we often create remedies for grade levels of students, not specific students. For example, if a third-grade class performs poorly on certain aspects of a state exam, the instructional program for third graders may change. However, the data that we use to make these changes are for students who are now in the fourth grade and not the third. In other words, the data that we are analyzing are old, and the improvements that we make are often applied to a different target group of learners.

Additionally, as we learned in Chapters 1 and 2, many teachers have not been trained to work with diverse student populations, especially academic language learners. As a result, it is likely that our decision making may be based on assumptions and not necessarily on what is really occurring and why. Take, for example, Jacob, our urban high school student in Massachusetts. Jacob's cultural background involves the belief that he should answer questions only when he is sure of the answer. Taking an educated guess is not his cultural way of being and acting. Jacob did poorly on the state mathematics exam. When his teachers pored over his results, they believed that he did not understand a number of concepts and figured that he would benefit from a state math assessment preparation class. Jacob passively agreed to this plan and subsequently did poorly on the state assessment again. A second review of his performance led to the teachers thinking that he should repeat the algebra course even though he had passed it. This is one example of how making decisions based on state assessment outcomes can often be misleading.

Let's look at another example. Bo's assessment results are reported in the total aggregate as well as the Asian subgroup of students. He is Chinese and comes from a home that carries academic language. He has a close group of peers who, like him, are from a strong academic language community. In the same district are a small but growing number of Chinese students who are what Yoshikawa (2011) refers to as citizens of undocumented immigrants. They are also academic language learners and do not have the same educational, socioeconomic, and critical school-matched experiences to draw from as Bo and his peers. However, since the majority of the Asian subgroup has done well on the state assessments, the growing population of academic language learners within the larger subgroup of Asians is not being noted.

Improvement of individual student outcomes is of concern to all educators. This is particularly true for educators of academic language learners. As we discussed in Chapter 1, while various initiatives and actions—including the civil rights movement, passage of the Elementary and Secondary Education Act in the 1960s, the charter school movement in the

1990s, and passage of NCLB in 2000—have attempted to improve student outcomes, underserved groups continue to be among the most underachieving and vulnerable segment of the student population at risk of failing. While improvements are being made, they are not occurring rapidly enough. Perhaps it is because we are not shining light in the right areas. This may be the result of our feeling, or actually being, pressured to respond to our students' performance on state tests, focusing too much on this element and not enough on the actual planning and delivery of our lessons and our analysis of their effectiveness.

Yes, it is important for us to understand the specifics of how academic language issues impact standardized testing. At the same time, the reality that a segment of our student population continues to do poorly speaks to the need to make data-driven decisions that are intentionally focused on what it is that we do when we teach. In other words, we must make informed decisions about our instructional programming for academic language learners. This requires that we look more closely at the means by which we plan and deliver high-quality instruction as well as school environments and family engagement activities.

The following reflection prompts have been separated for individual study and team study. Complete the prompt that applies to your particular context.

REFLECTION PROMPT FOR INDIVIDUAL STUDY

Time for Reflection:

Reflect on the following questions, and write a response.

- We have discussed a variety of challenges that occur in analyzing data. What steps have you taken or would you take to ensure that your data collection provides a more accurate picture of students, particularly academic language learners?

- How would these steps provide you with the information that you will need to respond more effectively to their learning needs?

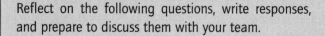

REFLECTION PROMPT FOR TEAM STUDY AND OUR-O-LOGUE

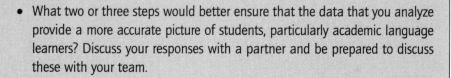

Time for Reflection:

Reflect on the following questions, write responses, and prepare to discuss them with your team.

- What two or three steps would better ensure that the data that you analyze provide a more accurate picture of students, particularly academic language learners? Discuss your responses with a partner and be prepared to discuss these with your team.

- Drawing from the ideas that you have developed, how would you share your plans with parents and involve them in the process?

USING THE FOUR-PRONGED FRAMEWORK FOR MAKING DATA-DRIVEN DECISIONS

Up until this point in this chapter, we have discussed the complexities of using state assessment data to inform our instruction. This is not to say that such data are not important. It is to say that using the data as a primary source for determining the improvements that are needed is not likely to advance student achievement and parent engagement. In response, the U.S. Department of Education is seeking a more effective means of assessment. It awarded funds to two multistate consortiums for this purpose: the Partnership for Assessment of Readiness for College and Careers (2012) and the Smarter Balanced Assessment Consortium (2012). Each is developing assessments that are intended to provide quicker and more effective means for understanding students' attainment of knowledge in English language arts/literacy and mathematics based on the Common Core State Standards (2012). While it is important to have a reliable and valid assessment system based on the knowledge and skills that students are expected to learn, it is even more critical that we have a system for understanding how to plan and deliver instruction and refine our practice so that academic language learners can flourish in school and parents can be partners in their child's education.

In the remainder of this chapter, we explore a variety of means for understanding and advancing student performance and family engagement as they relate to academic language learners. We explore the following question:

> How can we use the four-pronged framework to analyze and strengthen classroom, school, and parent-engagement communities?

Our four-pronged framework for improving student performance can greatly help in identifying and implementing the most effective types of classroom learning, school, and family engagement environments. It calls for looking at academic language learning from four different but interdependent, interconnected perspectives:

1. Learning as a sociocultural process

2. Learning as a developmental process

3. Learning as an academic process

4. Learning as a cognitive process

Our capacity to make data-driven decisions about lesson planning and delivery, the curriculum, and the strength of our parent/family partnerships should take into account these four components. When these are applied, we have a much better chance to build our awareness and intentionality about what is important to consider and include in our efforts to advance student achievement. How do we accomplish this goal? In the next segment of this chapter, we discuss how to employ observational rubrics and charts as key tools to use for individual and collaborative observation, reflection, and refinement of our practice.

Using Observational Rubrics to Inform Our Practice

Observational protocols are an effective means for understanding what is working and what needs strengthening (Calderón & Minaya-Rowe, 2011; Echevarria, Vogt, & Short, 2008). They are also helpful for individual as well as collaborative use. Several educators have used them extensively to improve or strengthen

- student performance,
- how we use data to make decisions,
- classroom instruction,
- parent–school engagement, and
- teaching practices (Zacarian, 2011; Zacarian & Haynes, 2012).

Using a rubric that is constructed from research-based best practices is important. It is also critical to use an approach that includes a sequential process of steps or stages and is collaborative and empowering. The Center for Research on Education, Diversity & Excellence (2002) and Teemant (2009) provide us with descriptors to reflect stages of professional growth (Figure 8.1).

The observational rubrics found at the end of this chapter labeled Resources A–D, excerpts of which can be seen in Figures 8.4–8.7, provide us with a means to measure the integration of the four prongs in our work. The format is drawn from my own observation rubrics, charts, and resources for measuring professional growth in integrating the four frames (Zacarian, 2011); rubrics created by the Center for Research on Education, Diversity & Excellence (2002) and Teemant (2009); and Pransky's (2008) research on culturally and linguistically diverse populations. In addition,

Figure 8.1 Stages of Professional Growth

Rubric
  Emerging
  Developing
  Enacting
  Integrating

Source: Adapted from Teemant (2009).

the contents are drawn from the research-based best practices presented in this book.

It is important to keep in mind that these rubrics are intended for professional growth and that growth for veteran as well as novice educators does not happen quickly. True integration of each of these elements takes time. Also, the rubrics should not be viewed as a means to an end. Rather, they should be used in a recursive process in which we continuously observe, reflect upon, and revise our practice so that we can meet the needs of our ever-changing student and family populations.

The rubric contains four primary sections, each representing one of the four prongs: the sociocultural frame, the academic literacy frame, the academic frame, and the cognitive thinking-to-learn frame. These are further separated to include the key research-based elements that were presented earlier in the book. For example, the rubric for the sociocultural frame has been separated to include a professional growth model for building relationships with students, connecting curriculum to students' lives, and engaging students in paired and cooperative group work. In addition, an important element of the rubrics is its infusion of parent engagement. Within each of the four prongs is a segment that is devoted to parent engagement. They reflect the research-based best practices discussed in Chapter 7.

The rubrics are intended for individuals as well as collaborative teams, coaches, peers, and mentors, as well as for supportive supervision in preservice and inservice settings. Ideally, they should be used to guide and supportively improve teachers' practice for the purpose of advancing student achievement and to strengthen parent–school partnerships. A helpful means for this type of work is to allocate time to use the rubrics to plan, deliver, analyze, and refine our practice individually and collaboratively. Figures 8.2 and 8.3 provide a description of this type of individual and collaborative recursive practice.

Figure 8.2 Application of the Protocol for Individual Use

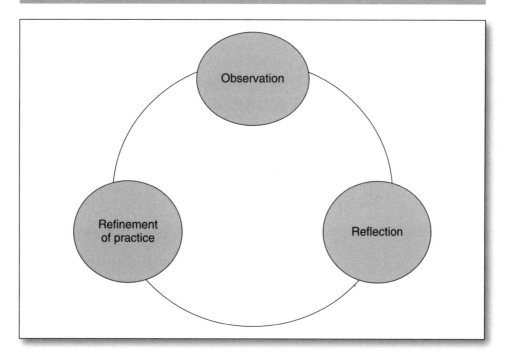

Figure 8.3 Application of the Protocol for a Collaborative Our-o-logue

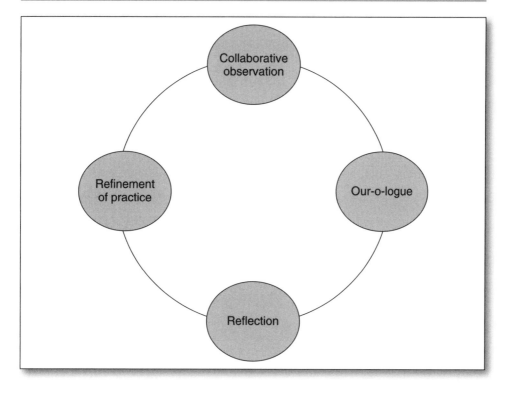

USING LOCAL FORMATIVE AND SUMMATIVE ASSESSMENTS

Evaluating the effectiveness of our learning, school, and family engagement environments must be a multidimensional process. Each of the four prongs is interdependent and interconnected with the other and offers us a helpful means for securing the type of comprehensive information that we need to make decisions about what we are doing and what we need to do.

The rubric should be used to guide the plans that we need to craft a lesson or activity. It is also intended to use for examining the successful delivery of a lesson as it is occurring as well as a unit of study after it has occurred. The rubric can also be used to plan, deliver, and assess the effectiveness of parent engagement activities. This includes using it for formative and summative assessments to ensure that what is occurring is effective. Let's examine how the rubrics in our book can be used for formative and summative assessments.

Formative Assessments

As educators, we know that we must continuously assess whether what we are doing is working. A common type of this assessment process occurs on the spot as a lesson or event, such as a parent conference, unfolds. It allows us to make quick shifts in what we are doing in the moment. For example, in Chapter 1, we met Lily, a kindergarten student, and Mrs. Fielding, Lily's teacher, and we learned about Lily's parents. We read that Lily's mother must drop her off at the front door of school as opposed to walking Lily to her classroom. We also learned that the primary means of communication between Mrs. Fielding and Lily's parents is in the form of written information including on topics such as "reading to your child" and "nutrition for your child." We also learned that Mrs. Fielding is concerned about Lily's progress and that she had hoped to discuss her concerns with Lily's parents. When they do not come for the parent conference, she wonders what she can do.

Using the Rubric for the Sociocultural Frame

Let's have a look at Figure 8.4 to explore how to use the rubric. In the section labeled Builds Relationships With Parents, we see that there are four stages. (The complete versions of all rubrics referenced in this chapter can be found at the end of the chapter.)

Figure 8.4 Excerpt From the Rubric for the Sociocultural Frame

	Emerging	Developing	Enacting	Integrating
Builds relationships with parents	• Connects with parents by conducting parent conferences to report student progress and Open House to report class curriculum, routines, and activities • Communicates with parents by providing information	• Has some level of understanding of some students' parents • Makes some connections with some parents beyond typical routine school activities and is attempting to build relationships	• Is developing understanding of most students' parents • Has begun to connect personal, social, cultural, and world knowledge of parents and is infusing these into some social activities • Infuses this understanding to encourage parents to participate in school • Is beginning to create routine activities for parent participation in more than routine events to support their child's learning	• Personally connects with each student's family • Empathetically understands each family • Infuses this understanding into the learning environment • Continuously welcomes and promotes parent engagement • Creates socially welcoming gatherings where parents participate actively • Helps families see value in learning and their child's future

Mrs. Fielding attempts to make contact with parents. She sends information home and schedules a parent conference.

The Emerging stage states the following:

- Makes infrequent attempts to reach out to family
- Connects with parents by conducting typical routinized events such as parent conferences and Open House to report student progress
- Communicates with parents by providing information
- Provides limited encouragement for communication

As we review the next stage, it states that the teacher is making some connections with some parents beyond the routine school activities that generally occur and is attempting to build relationships with them. Mrs. Fielding is at the *Emerging* stage of development, and there are many opportunities for growth. For example, she might hold a social event such as an early morning breakfast, afterschool pot luck supper, or other social gathering to build relationships with families.

The following reflection prompts have been separated for individual study and team study. Complete the prompt that applies to your particular context.

REFLECTION PROMPT FOR INDIVIDUAL STUDY

Time for Reflection:

Reflect on the following question, and write a response.

- What social activity might Mrs. Fielding do to build relationships with families? Create at least one activity and describe it.

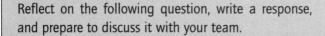

REFLECTION PROMPT FOR TEAM STUDY AND OUR-O-LOGUE

Time for Reflection:

Reflect on the following question, write a response, and prepare to discuss it with your team.

- With a partner, what are two or three additional activities that you might encourage Mrs. Fielding to do?

A second important step in planning to use formative assessments is thinking about what's important to consider for making moment-to-moment decisions. The rubric can be a helpful guide for this purpose. For example, it is important to learn about our students' and their families' personal, social, cultural, and world experiences. The social gathering event can be a helpful means for engaging in this behavior, and an individual or collaborative review of the rubric and our application of this frame can be a helpful means for strengthening our work.

Using the Rubric to Help Students Develop Strong Language and Literacy Skills

Let's have a look at Figure 8.5, an excerpt from the rubric for developing strong academic language and literacy skills.

In Chapter 4, we met Eric, a student in Mrs. Shumway's eighth-grade English class. Mrs. Shumway has teamed with a social studies teacher to support the class's study of the Civil War. Her class is reading the social studies text and the novel *The Red Badge of Courage* (Crane, 1895). She has separated her class into small learning groups, each of which represents

Figure 8.5 Excerpt From the Rubric for Academic Language and Literacy

	Emerging	Developing	Enacting	Integrating

Pays attention to students' language and literacy development	• Instruction primarily teacher-led (lecture style & whole class instruction)
	• Flow of interaction is generally teacher-student-teacher whereby a small number of students speak or are called on to speak.
	• Instruction is primarily driven by curriculum
	• Vocabulary instruction is driven by text and generally in the form of single word lists that are not categorized contextually
		• Appropriate language (listening, speaking, reading, writing) may be explicitly modeled
		• Engages students in brief, repetitive, or drill-like reading, writing, or speaking activities
		• Begins to identify subject-specific language patterns
		• Begins to define key academic language and vocabulary that is routinely used in subject matter and school; provides some instruction in this realm
			• More consistently aware of students' academic language learning needs
			• More consistently taking time to teach academic language learners in specific ways:
			  1. Making note of subject-specific language patterns and providing more consistent direct instruction in them
			  2. Supporting students in understanding author intent
			  3. More consistent use of student interaction using context-driven academic language
			  4. Beginning to build rich vocabulary instruction targeted to enhancing more descriptive language use (including academic conversations that make use of Tier 2 words)
			  5. Word walls, table mats, handouts, and other devices sometimes used to support conversations in academic language
				• Designs and enacts instructional activities that consistently generate the type of communication that is expected (e.g., speaking, writing), and continuously supports students' communication skills in all four domains (listening, speaking, reading, writing)
				• Posts key communication terms, words, idioms, and phrases to support students' capacity to communicate in the language of content (e.g., the ways in which science experiments are expressed)
				• Helps students use language more precisely
				• Routinely uses categorized word walls, table mats, handouts, and other devices to support conversations in academic language

a family from either the North or South, and tasked them to write personal letters between a family member who is fighting in the war and someone who remained at home. Mrs. Shumway pays close attention to Eric's stage of literacy development. She also models the type of letter writing that she expects and provides her students with several model samples. She posts key communication terms for the writing activity to support her students' understanding of the historical time period and personal narrative writing. She also uses a number of visuals, including graphic organizers. She engages her students in talking about their group's letters. She carefully assigns homework tasks that provide her students with additional practice opportunities. She also is in constant communication with parents about this unit of study. As a culminating activity, she has invited parents to come to her classroom to see their children's letters. The activity occurs before, during, and after school to accommodate parents' availability.

The following reflection prompts have been separated for individual study and team study. Complete the prompt that applies to your particular context.

REFLECTION PROMPT FOR INDIVIDUAL STUDY

Time for Reflection:

Reflect on the following questions, and write responses.

- Review the excerpt from the academic language literacy frame rubric in Figure 8.5 to determine the stage that Mrs. Shumway represents. What stage of professional development would you assign Mrs. Shumway? Why?

(Continued)

(Continued)

- Create an additional academic literacy learning activity that Mrs. Shumway might include that would help her to advance to the next stage of professional development or, if you believe that she is at the integrating stage, to maintain this stage of professional development.

REFLECTION PROMPT FOR TEAM STUDY AND OUR-O-LOGUE

Time for Reflection:

Reflect on the following questions, write responses, and prepare to discuss them with your team.

- With a partner, come to agreement on the stage of development that Mrs. Shumway represents in this element of the academic language and literacy rubric.

- Design two to three additional activities that she might do to advance her stage of professional development or, if you believe that she is at the integrating stage, to maintain this stage of professional development using this rubric element as a guide.

Using the Rubric to Put the Academic/Curriculum Frame Into Practice

Let's have a look at Jacob's ninth-grade algebra class. We begin as the class is unfolding. Jacob's teacher, Mrs. Littleton, begins the lesson by asking students to write the formula for the quadratic equation in their notebooks. As she walks around the room to check to see that this occurs, she sees that several students have written either the wrong formula or nothing at all. Quickly realizing that she has to review the formula with her class, Mrs. Littleton alters her lesson plan. She walks to the white board and puts three formulas on the board. She says, "One of these is correct, and the others are not. I need to consider which two are wrong. How would I do this? Well, here is what I know about the quadratic equation . . ."

She continues to share her thoughts aloud with her students and then asks for a volunteer to select the correct formula. After she receives the student's selection, she asks the rest of the class if they agree with it. Everyone agrees with the answer. When this is done, she erases the incorrect formulas and tells her students to write the one remaining correct formula in their notebooks and to label it "Quadratic Equation." As they do this, Mrs. Littleton walks around her classroom to see that they have noted the correct formula. She quietly stops to talk with some of her students to affirm that they have written the right formula. This type of on-the-spot formative assessment provides Mrs. Littleton with the opportunities that she believes are needed to individualize instruction and support the comprehension and application of content. If we look closely at Figure 8.6, we can examine what Mrs. Littleton is doing to support her students' learning.

Figure 8.6 Excerpt From the Rubric for the Academic-Curricular Frame

	Emerging	Developing	Enacting	Integrating
Provides modeling and practice opportunities	• Provides very limited modeling or practice opportunities to complete academic tasks and assignments	• Occasionally models completed product, behaviors, thinking processes, or procedures necessary for a task • Gives students little practice time to learn	• Is beginning to routinely provide a model of completed product that students make, or models the behaviors, thinking processes, or procedures necessary for the task • Gives students more ample practice time	• Provides a model of completed product that students then make, or models the behavior, thinking processes, or procedures necessary for the task and assists students during practice • Gives students sufficient practice time to fully learn material

We see that she does not provide her students with ample modeling of the behaviors, thinking processes, and/or procedures needed or practice time, placing her at the *Developing* stage. She will need to expand the number of practice opportunities that she provides her students.

The following reflection prompts have been separated for individual study and team study. Complete the prompt that applies to your particular context.

REFLECTION PROMPT FOR INDIVIDUAL STUDY

Time for Reflection:

Reflect on the following and write a response.

• Formative assessments help us know whether our plans are successful and that we need to make changes when they are not. Formative assessments also are good vehicles for assessing student learning. Create two to three additional activities and accompanying formative on-the-spot assessments that Mrs. Littleton might use to assess her lesson's effectiveness and to check for student understanding.

REFLECTION PROMPT FOR TEAM STUDY AND OUR-O-LOGUE

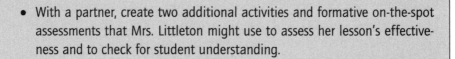

Time for Reflection:

Reflect on the following prompts, write responses, and prepare to discuss them with your team.

- With a partner, create two additional activities and formative on-the-spot assessments that Mrs. Littleton might use to assess her lesson's effectiveness and to check for student understanding.

(Continued)

(Continued)

- Create a lesson activity on a topic of your choosing. Design two formative on-the-spot assessments that you will use to determine its effectiveness.

Summative Assessments

Summative assessments are commonly used at the midpoint of a unit of study or after it is completed, at midterm, and at the end of the term. They are provided to determine how much learning has taken place and whether standards have been met. State assessments are a type of summative assessment, as are midterm, final, and unit exams in specific subjects. For example, at the end of the term, Mrs. Littleton will be giving her students a final exam that will assess, among other things, their understanding of the quadratic equation.

What is critical is that students receive an explicit instructional program that is connected to their personal lives (the sociocultural prong), their level of literacy development (the language prong), their content learning needs (the academic prong), and, finally, the thinking skills that are needed to take summative assessments (the cognitive prong). Thus the data that guide decisions must be focused on these four interdependent lenses.

To support our understanding of how this might be applied, let's revisit Chapter 6 and our exploration of the cognitive thinking-to-learn frame. In it, we met Mrs. Nelson, who is working on a fourth-grade social studies unit on recent African immigrant groups. In the chapter, we were given an example what Mrs. Nelson might do to engage her students in academic conversations to express their understanding about the African immigrant group they are studying. Mrs. Nelson wants to engage in a self-study of her practice at the midpoint of this unit of study. As she engages in this process, she determines that she is at the *Developing* stage in this area (see Figure 8.7). She does this because she acknowledges the importance and wants to make better use of sentence prompts and sentence responses in her practice to improve her student's academic performance.

The following reflection prompts have been separated for individual study and team study. Look over Figure 8.8, and then complete the prompt that applies to your particular context.

Figure 8.7 First Excerpt From the Rubric for the Cognitive Thinking-to-Learn Frame

	Emerging	Developing	Enacting	Integrating
Instructional conversation incorporates challenging, thought-provoking dialogues	• Instruction is primarily lecture led • Small portion of the lesson requires interaction but this is primarily in response to questions that require a one-word response for information	• Is beginning to use academic conversations that make use of some sentence prompts and sentence responses that engage students in thinking-to-learn activities • Is beginning to make use of questioning, listening, or rephrasing to elicit some student talk • Is beginning to converse with students, and students are using academic thinking-to-learn talk during some of the lesson.	• Is beginning to require students to converse in pairs and small groups on an academic topic • Makes regular use of sentence prompts and responses that explicitly make connections to text to engage students in meaningful academic conversations	• Designs and enacts instructional conversations with clear academic goals • Listens carefully to assess and assist student understanding, *and* questions students about their views, judgments, or rationales • Routinely uses sentence prompts and response starters to connect student talk to academic content learning/language • Students engage in high rates of talk

Figure 8.8 Second Excerpt From the Rubric for the Cognitive Thinking-to-Learn Frame

	Emerging	Developing	Enacting	Integrating
Involves parents/ families in supporting their child's thinking-to-learn skills	• Primarily provides parents with information about their child's learning, not *how* their child is learning	• Is beginning to share the purpose of learning activities • Is beginning to share learning objectives; these generally continue to be informational without much parent interaction	• Shares purpose of learning activities • Shares learning objectives and what students will do to learn on a more regular basis • Holds some parent meetings (e.g., family night) to discuss learning goals and activities • Is beginning to create homework activities that all parents can do to support their child's learning	• Continuously and routinely shares purpose of learning activities with parents • Continuously provides learning objectives and what students will do to learn • Holds parent meetings to explain learning goals and activities • Infuses learning activities that can be done at home to support learning • Holds family events that supports thinking-to-learn goals

REFLECTION PROMPT FOR INDIVIDUAL STUDY

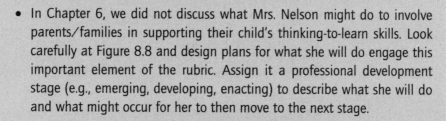

Time for Reflection:

Reflect on the following and write responses.
   Summative assessments help us determine how much learning has taken place and whether standards have been met. They also help us plan how to involve parents and families in their child's learning.

- In Chapter 6, we did not discuss what Mrs. Nelson might do to involve parents/families in supporting their child's thinking-to-learn skills. Look carefully at Figure 8.8 and design plans for what she will do engage this important element of the rubric. Assign it a professional development stage (e.g., emerging, developing, enacting) to describe what she will do and what might occur for her to then move to the next stage.

- Design one or two activities that are focused on one or two of the bullets in this part of the rubric.

REFLECTION PROMPT FOR TEAM STUDY AND OUR-O-LOGUE

Time for Reflection:

Reflect on the following questions, write responses, and prepare to discuss them with your team.

(Continued)

(Continued)

Summative assessments help us determine how much learning has taken place and whether standards have been met. They also help us plan for involving parents and families in their child's learning.

- Revisit Chapter 6. Using the elements of the rubric found in Figure 8.8, describe what Mrs. Nelson might do to involve parents/families in supporting their child's thinking-to-learn skills.

- Describe the stage of growth that this represents.

- Describe what she will do to move to the next level of professional development.

Selecting a Collaborative Data Analysis Group to Understand the Learning Needs of Academic Language Learners

While individual observation, reflection, and refinement of practice are important to do, collaborative inquiry is a powerful means for understanding the diverse needs of academic language learners. Referring back to our initial call for an our-o-logue as opposed to a my-o-logue about learners and learning, a collaborative dialogue is essential for gathering high-quality data about our students and their families and our capacity to analyze the data effectively. Convening a team to engage in this work supports its being a collaborative and not a solo process. It speaks to the heart of what we do as public school educators—we share responsibility for teaching and reaching every student. Drawing from Zacarian (2011), to do this requires that we collaboratively examine the following:

1. the curriculum and instructional materials that we use to teach and their capacity to build connections with students' personal, cultural, world, and academic experiences (i.e., what works and what is needed)

2. how the curriculum, instructional materials, and the ways in which we deliver lessons connects with our students' literacy learning needs

3. the method by which our academic goals will be achieved

4. the ways in which we are teaching our students to think to learn

5. most important, the overall effectiveness of our instructional programming with academic language learners

A collaborative group is critical to this work (Love et al., 2008). Ideally, it should include participants with depth of knowledge about the focal students and their families. While it is important that the group be small enough so that everyone is an active member and has an important role to play, it should not be at the expense of missing the important role of a knowledgeable "insider" who is a representative of the focal group. For example, earlier in the chapter, we learned of a group of Chinese students who are not performing well. They are citizen children of undocumented immigrants and have not had the same school-matched literacy experiences as have the majority of Chinese students in this subgroup. A team member who is familiar with these specific students and their families can greatly help in securing a more appropriate instructional approach.

One of the most helpful means of collecting data about student progress and parent engagement is to do this as a collaborative effort in which more than one person determines the type of data that will be collected, how, when, under what circumstances, and the methods by which data will be analyzed. This could not be truer for the protocols that we use to assess academic language learners. Many of us may be working in communities where the dominant student population carries academic language and the minority are learners of academic language. In addition, the textbooks and pace that we use to teach and their accompanying assessment protocols may be based on an assumption that all students carry academic language.

In each of these examples, we often do not consider the pitfalls of what Daniel Kahneman refers to as the *law of small numbers*. Kahneman, a renowned winner of the Nobel Prize for economics and author of *Thinking Fast and Slow* (2011), claims that we often formulate hypotheses based on limited information and then make broad sweeping assumptions based on this small set of data.

The following reflection prompts have been separated for individual study and team study. Complete the prompt that applies to your particular context.

REFLECTION PROMPT FOR INDIVIDUAL STUDY

Time for Reflection:

Reflect on the following question, and write a response.

- Think about the community of educators, community service practitioners, parents, students, and other stakeholders in your particular context. Who might you involve in this collaborative inquiry group? What are the concerns that you might have about this collaborative group (given the members that you have selected), and how might you address these concerns?

REFLECTION PROMPT FOR TEAM STUDY AND OUR-O-LOGUE

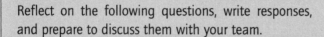

Time for Reflection:

Reflect on the following questions, write responses, and prepare to discuss them with your team.

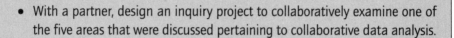

- With a partner, design an inquiry project to collaboratively examine one of the five areas that were discussed pertaining to collaborative data analysis.

- Describe specific members of the school community, the local community's service agencies, parents, students, and other stakeholders that you will include in this collaborative inquiry group.

- What might be some of the obstacles for collaborative involvement? How might you address these?

UNDERSTANDING THE PHASES OF COLLABORATIVE INQUIRY

It is helpful to understand collaborative inquiry as a process that includes four phases:

1. Collaborative understanding of observational rubrics

2. Coming to agreement about the data that will be collected

3. Collaborative analysis of the data to determine needs

4. Collectively addressing the needs that are identified

Collaborative Understanding of Observational Rubrics

The observational rubrics found in Resources A–D provide specific language and descriptors for integrating the four prongs into our practice. While we might want to rush into using the rubrics quickly, it is important to take the time needed to use them successfully. To do this well, a group of teachers might collaborate for the purpose of reviewing and becoming familiar with the rubric. Indeed, there are many means for gaining the knowledge and skills that are needed to use these effectively. It is beneficial to make this an active learning process. One way for a group to do this is to look closely at one element and the different stages within the element, and discuss how these stages might be evidenced in practice. It is also helpful to collaboratively observe this element in action. This helps to build consensus about the specific stages of professional development that are observed and more.

Coming to Agreement About the Data That Will Be Collected

While Rubrics A–D have been written in a specific order, it is important to consider how they can be used the most effectively and supportively in your particular context. For example, some of us may use them in the order that they are presented as part of a book study or participation in a college course. We might follow the chapter-by-chapter sequence of our book and the arrangement of the rubrics as part of this step-by-step study. Others may select the prong and the elements within it that are the most relevant for their work. Still others may select one element within a prong. Whatever is chosen, groups must first come to agreement about what will be collected, when it will be collected, and the collection method that will be used. In addition, whatever order is used, plans should be made to observe each element, as they are interdependent.

Using Observation Charts

It is important to collect comprehensive data to ensure that the findings are accurate. An example of doing this process poorly would be a peer observer who spends a few minutes in a classroom and uses his/her limited observations to make sweeping judgments. In a real sense, the process of observation is intended to capture as full a picture as possible.

Observation charts are essential for noting what is observed. Resources E–H have been created for this purpose. There are many ways to collect observation data. One is to collaboratively settle on a focus element and observe one event, such as a math class in one classroom, multiple times. Another is to observe lessons in many classrooms. Once a plan is established for how the data will be collected, it will be much more purposeful and intentional.

Let's look at a team of six high school teachers who want to strengthen their teaching practices with academic language learners. We begin as they are reviewing Rubrics A–D. Mrs. Passo, the group's facilitator, suggests that they select one element to help them to get started using the rubrics. The group reviews the four prongs and elements within each and settles on one from Rubric D, the thinking-to-learn prong: *Instructional conversation incorporates challenging, thought-provoking dialogues.* Then they look closely at each of the stages within it and discuss how each might be represented in practice. When they complete their discussion, Mrs. Passo suggests that they move to the next phase of their work—data collection. One of the members, Mrs. Johanson, suggests that they collect data through peer-peer observation. The group agrees with this plan and separates into pairs. They conclude their meeting with the plan of observing each other three times during the next two weeks.

Referring to Chapter 6 (about learning as a cognitive process) and Rubric D, Mrs. Passo and Mrs. Johanson observe each other during a lesson activity. Each writes detailed observation notes and assigns a stage of professional development on the chart found in Resource H. Figures 8.9 and 8.10 reflect the stage that each assigned during the three observations.

The collaborative group meets after observations are completed. With the rubrics and completed observation charts in hand, the group discusses their findings. They find that the group is mostly at the developing stage of professional development in this element. This leads to a purposeful discussion about what they will do to strengthen their practice

Figure 8.9 Mrs. Passo's Observation of Mrs. Johanson

Stage of professional development	Emerging	Developing	Enacting	Integrating
Instructional conversation incorporates challenging, thought-provoking dialogues		//	/	

Figure 8.10 Mrs. Johanson's Observation of Mrs. Passo

Stage of professional development	Emerging	Developing	Enacting	Integrating
Instructional conversation incorporates challenging, thought-provoking dialogues		///		

and plan for further observation. The observation charts found in Resources E–H are intended for this type of self, peer, and collaborative analyses to identify trends and, most important, the professional growth that is needed.

PUTTING DATA-DRIVEN DECISIONS INTO PRACTICE

- Using a four-pronged approach for making data-driven decisions
- Using the research-based rubric furnished in this chapter to observe, reflect, and refine practice to strengthen student performance and parent engagement
- Using the observational rubric individually and collaboratively
- Using a collaborative approach to best understand students' learning needs and the best means for engaging parents as partners

SUMMARY

In this chapter, we discussed the complexities of making data-driven decisions based on state assessment results. We learned the importance of using observational rubrics for understanding, reflecting on, and refining our practice. We were introduced to an observational rubric that is based on the four-pronged framework—including the sociocultural, academic language/literacy, academic-curricular, and cognitive thinking-to-learn frames—as it applies to student learning and parent engagement.

CONCLUSION

While teaching is a highly evaluative profession (think of all of the on-the-spot decisions that we make on a daily basis!), we must prepare ourselves to create a comprehensive picture that accounts for the four prongs that we have explored throughout this book. When this is done frequently and with consistency, we can address our students and their families and, importantly, our work more effectively.

Indeed, the process of mastering academic language is a comprehensive and recursive process. It requires that we understand the application of the four prongs presented in this book and integrate them into our practice. At a foundational level, the four prongs—sociocultural, academic language/literacy, academic-curriculum, and cognitive thinking-to-learn—truly make a difference in how we think and what we do to advance achievement so that all learners can carry academic language and successfully perform in school and beyond.

Resource A. Rubric for the Sociocultural Frame

Grounds learning by (1) building strong relationships with students and families, (2) connecting curriculum with issues that are socially relevant for students', and (3) drawing from students' sociocultural strengths

Stage of professional development	Emerging	Developing	Enacting	Integrating
Builds relationships with students	• Subject matter is primary focus (e.g., curriculum to be covered and academic tasks related to it)	• Has some level of understanding of some of the students • Is beginning to infuse this understanding into the learning environment	• Is developing understanding of most students • Has begun to infuse student interests in learning • Is building connections and relationships with students • Helps most students see value in learning and beyond	• Empathetically understands each student • Knows students' interests • Personally connects with each student • Infuses this understanding into the learning environment • Helps students see value in learning and their future
Builds relationships with parents	• Connects with parents by conducting typical routinized events such as parent conferences and Open House to report student progress • Communicates with parents by providing information	• Has some level of understanding of some students' parents • Makes some connections with some parents beyond typical routine school activities and is attempting to build relationships	• Is developing understanding of most students' parents • Has begun to connect personal, social, cultural, and world knowledge of parents and is infusing these into some social activities • Infuses this understanding to encourage parents to participate in school	• Personally connects with each student's family • Empathetically understands each family • Infuses this understanding into the learning environment • Continuously welcomes and promotes parent engagement

Stage of professional development	Emerging	Developing	Enacting	Integrating
			• Is beginning to create routine activities for parent participation in more than routine events to support their child's learning	• Creates socially welcoming gatherings where parents participate actively • Helps families see value in learning and their child's future
Connects curriculum with students' lives to create a context-rich learning environment	• Primarily connects learning to curriculum	• Makes some attempt to ground lessons in students' prior personal, cultural, and world experiences	• Makes more consistent connections to students' personal, cultural, and world experiences • Helps students see meaning and value in the content	• Grounds learning in students' personal, cultural, and world experiences • Routinely supports students in taking a critical stance on socially relevant issues and infuses this connection into the curriculum to create a context-rich environment
Connects curriculum with parents' lives to support learning in and out of school	• Learning is primarily connected to curriculum	• Some attempt to ground lessons in home connections • Minimal contact with parents to help ground lessons and learning experiences in families' lives	• More consistent connection made to families' personal, cultural, and world experiences • Helps parents see meaning and value in child's learning	• Ensures that all learning is grounded and connected to parents' lives, with multiple socially relevant connections made between home and school • Parents are regularly included in student learning

(Continued)

(Continued)

Stage of professional development	Emerging	Developing	Enacting	Integrating
Engages students in paired and small group work	• Lecture or whole-class instruction is primary mode with occasional allowance for students to ask or respond to questions	• Engages students to mainly work independently • Assigns some special group projects • Makes some attempts to group students according to skill level • Provides students with limited instruction in productive pair or small-group work	• Some instruction is provided about the process and product of pair and group work • Is attempting to use more flexible grouping • Is beginning to assign roles for pair and group work • Includes at least two interaction modes (e.g., pair, small group) in each lesson	• Consistently uses flexible grouping strategies • Models expectations of process and task • Assigns students varied, rotating roles as appropriate • Continuously presents opportunities for students to provide feedback about their learning as well as group process and product/task

Resource B. Rubric for the Academic Language and Literacy Frame

Helps students develop strong language and literacy skills and ensures that parent communication is accessible			
Stage of professional development	**Emerging**	**Developing**	**Enacting**	**Integrating**

Pays attention to students' language and literacy development	• Instruction primarily teacher led (lecture style and whole class instruction)
	• Flow of interaction is generally teacher-student-teacher whereby a small number of students speak or are called on to speak)
	• Instruction is primarily driven by curriculum
	• Vocabulary instruction is driven by text and generally in form of single word lists that are not categorized contextually
		• Appropriate language (listening, speaking, reading, writing) may be explicitly modeled
		• Engages students in brief, repetitive, or drill-like reading, writing, or speaking activities
		• Begins to identify subject-specific language patterns
		• Begins to define key academic language and vocabulary that is routinely used in subject matter and school; provides some instruction in this realm
			• More consistently aware of students' academic language learning needs
			• More consistently taking time to teach academic language learners in specific ways:
			  1. Making note of subject-specific language patterns and providing more consistent direct instruction in them
			  2. Supporting students in understanding author intent
			  3. More consistent use of student
				• Designs and enacts instructional activities that consistently generate the type of communication that is expected (e.g., speaking, writing), and continuously supports students' communication skills in all four domains (listening, speaking, reading, writing)
				• Posts key communication terms, words, idioms, and phrases to support students' capacity to communicate in the language of content (e.g., the ways in which science experiments are expressed)

(Continued)

(Continued)

Stage of professional development	Emerging	Developing	Enacting	Integrating
			interaction using context-driven academic language 4. Beginning to build rich vocabulary instruction targeted to enhancing more descriptive language use (including academic conversations that make use of Tier 2 words) 5. Word walls, table mats, handouts, and other devices sometimes used to support conversations in academic language	• Helps students use language more precisely • Routinely uses categorized word walls, table mats, handouts, and other devices to support conversations in academic language
Makes learning understandable	• Generally speaks quickly, with mostly sophisticated language • Uses few visuals or grounding experiences	• Sometimes repeats or rephrases some things • May use visuals, but these are not fully connected to content learning goals • Some attempts made to engage students in understanding academic talk	• Is beginning to use visuals and authentic experiences as well as graphic organizers • Uses a few techniques for fostering comprehension of academic talk • Some evidence of supplemental materials • Teacher language reflects an understanding of students' language/literacy levels	• Uses visual, authentic experiences and graphic organizers to scaffold comprehension • Teacher language reflects an understanding of students' language/literacy levels • Uses multiple techniques to foster comprehension of academic talk • Routinely uses supplemental materials

Stage of professional development	Emerging	Developing	Enacting	Integrating
Models and provides consistent practice opportunities	• Provides verbal directions expecting students to begin working after listening to these • Provides little practice time	• Models behaviors, thinking processes, or procedures with some opportunity for students to practice	• Provides a model of completed product that students then make, or models the behaviors, thinking processes, or procedures necessary for the task • Gives students more practice time	• Provides a model of a completed product that students then make, or models the behavior, thinking processes, or procedures necessary for the task, and assists students during practice tasks • Provides students with sufficient practice time and check-ins to learn material
Assigns homework and assesses based on students' level of literacy	• Assigns same homework to all students • Formative and summative assessments are the same for all students	• Makes some accommodations for students' various literacy levels	• Is beginning to design assessments and homework assignments based on students' varied literacy levels • Has at least one interim (formative) assessment activity during a lesson, or a time for reflection at end of lesson	• Designs and implements formative and summative assessments and homework based on students' developmental literacy levels using multiple sources and adapted texts to support students in listening, speaking, reading, and writing at a level a bit beyond their current literacy level

(Continued)

(Continued)

Stage of professional development	Emerging	Developing	Enacting	Integrating
				• Has at least one interim (formative) assessment activity during lesson and/or a time for metacognitive reflection at end of lesson
Understands parents' academic language level	• Communicates with parents in written mode (primarily informational, regarding school events or subject-specific information) using sophisticated language and expectation that parents are carriers of academic language and will communicate in similar fashion	• Attempts to understand parents' different academic language learning levels • Is beginning to communicate with parents in modes other than informational • Is beginning to involve parents in activities related to academic language, such as with home learning packets.	• More consistently communicates with parents in language that they understand • More consistently communicates with parents about academic language learning activities • More intentionally involves parents in activities related to academic language, such as with home learning packets	• Consistently communicates with parents in comprehensible language • Integrates home–school activities that relate to academic language learning

Resource C. Rubric for the Academic-Curricular Frame

Stage of professional development	Emerging	Developing	Enacting	Integrating
Helps students develop strong academic/curricular skills and connects parents to what (academic curriculum) their child is learning				
Uses clear overarching unit and day's learning and language objectives	• States general objective aloud • May display some objectives in varied locations • May copy an objective from state or local standard (i.e., written in sophisticated language) • May state or post objectives without explanation	• Attempts to write objectives in student-friendly, accessible language • Displays overarching unit objectives at times • Displays day's learning objective at times • Displays what students will do to learn (e.g., listening, speaking, reading, writing activities) at times	• Routinely displays unit objectives, day's content objectives (what students will learn and be able to do), and language (how students will use language to reach the content goal) • States most language objectives clearly and in student-friendly language • Draws students' attention to objectives at beginning, transition points, OR end of lesson	• Defines and displays clearly articulated unit objectives and day's learning and language objectives in student-friendly language • Directs student attention to unit and day's learning and language objectives at beginning, during, and end of lesson • Uses language goals that reflect process and product
Provides effective vocabulary instruction	• Displays limited vocabulary • Does not provide intentional vocabulary instruction	• Gives students lists of words to memorize in simple worksheets for practice • Does not highlight important vocabulary before lessons	• Is beginning to post key content vocabulary but is not yet organized in ways that support student learning • Is starting to do more content vocabulary practice • Highlights important vocabulary before lessons	• Posts key content vocabulary in organized ways • Provides ample opportunities for students to practice vocabulary to "own" it

(Continued)

(Continued)

Stage of professional development	Emerging	Developing	Enacting	Integrating
Provides challenging activities	• Most activities rely on repetition, recall, emphasizing factual or procedural information	• Teaches some challenging material but primarily relies on rote repetition, recall, or duplication of information	• Is beginning to design and enact activities with some standards/expectations and performance feedback • Is beginning to assist students in development of more complex thinking	• Designs and enacts challenging activities with clear standards, expectations, and performance feedback • Assists students in developing more complex thinking by engaging them in academic conversations that use the language of content
Provides modeling and practice opportunities	• Provides very limited modeling or practice opportunities to complete academic tasks and assignments	• Occasionally models completed product, behaviors, thinking processes, or procedures necessary for a task • Gives students little practice time to learn	• Is beginning to routinely provide a model of completed product that students make, or models the behaviors, thinking processes, or procedures necessary for the task • Gives students more ample practice time	• Provides a model of completed product that students then make, or models the behavior, thinking processes, or procedures necessary for the task and assists students during practice • Gives students sufficient practice time to fully learn material

Stage of professional development	Emerging	Developing	Enacting	Integrating
Involves parents/families in their child's academic-curricular learning	• Engages in limited communication with parents about what their child is learning, generally confined to reports each semester (e.g., report card) or information provided at Open House	• Is beginning to reach out to parents to provide more connections to what their child is learning • Attempts to build connections between what is being studied and home • Makes some attempts to involve parents in their child's learning	• More consistently reaches out to parents/family about what their child is learning • Invites parents to participate in learning at times • Builds connections between curriculum and home; learning activities beginning to reflect these connections • Attempts to provide engagement, including reading workshop, family math nights, parent-run study centers, and college-career nights	• Consistently reaches out to parents/family about what their child is learning • Parents routinely participate in learning • Connects curriculum and home • Includes multiple activities for engaging parents in curriculum, including reading workshop, family math nights, parent-run study centers, and college-career nights

Resource D. Rubric for the Cognitive Thinking-to-Learn Frame

Helps students develop strong cognitive thinking-to-learn skills and shares these with parents				
Stage of professional development	Emerging	Developing	Enacting	Integrating
Provides cognitive skill development to understand how we use language to express thinking	• Gives students work that primarily conveys facts and information (the lowest level of Bloom's taxonomy and only one of Halliday's seven language functions)	• Is beginning to teach explicit thinking skills, making note of Bloom's taxonomy and Halliday's seven language functions, but only some of these are taught and evidenced in a lesson	• More consistently includes Bloom's taxonomy and Halliday's language functions in lessons • Intentionally teaches thinking skills, but within the content itself and not as intentional as needed • Content tasks and assessment reflect higher levels of Bloom's taxonomy	• Intentionally teaches thinking skills that students need within the content and activities • Uses thinking-to-learn activities drawn from students' background knowledge • Engages students across all levels of Bloom's taxonomy (remembering, understanding, applying, analyzing, evaluating, creating) and Halliday's seven language functions
Instructional conversation incorporates challenging, thought-provoking dialogues	• Instruction is primarily lecture led • Small portion of the lesson requires interaction that is primarily in response to questions that require a one-word or few-word response for information and includes some or all students	• Is beginning to use oral academic conversations that make use of some academic sentence prompts and sentence responses that engage students in thinking-to-learn activities	• Is beginning to require students to converse in pairs and small groups on an academic topic • Makes regular use of sentence prompts and responses that explicitly make connections to text to engage students in meaningful academic conversations	• Designs and enacts instructional conversations with clear academic goals • Listens carefully to assess and assist student understanding, and questions students about their views, judgments, or rationales

Stage of professional development	Emerging	Developing	Enacting	Integrating
		• Is beginning to make use of questioning, listening, or rephrasing to elicit some student talk • Is beginning to converse with students, and students are using academic thinking-to-learn talk during some of the lesson		• Routinely uses sentence prompts and response starters to connect student talk to academic content learning/language • Students engage in high rates of talk
Uses visual organizers to support thinking-to-learn	• Uses limited OR many visual organizers that do not systematically support thinking • Provides no or limited instruction about how visual organizers are used	• Is beginning to use more visuals to convey specific types of thinking • Provides limited instruction for using visual organizers	• Uses organizers to support specific types of thinking (e.g., brainstorming, describing, sequencing, comparing/contrasting) • Teaches students how to use visual organizers • Displays graphic organizers with explanation of what each is used to do	• Uses organizers systematically to support specific types of thinking consistently • Provides direct, explicit instruction to use visual organizers to think to learn • Engages others in the school and district in use of the same organizers to allow for consistent thinking-to-learn among student population

(Continued)

(Continued)

Stage of professional development	Emerging	Developing	Enacting	Integrating
Involves parents/families in supporting their child's thinking-to-learn skills	• Primarily provides parents with information about their child's learning, not *how* their child is learning	• Is beginning to share the purpose of learning activities • Is beginning to share learning objectives. These generally continue to be informational without much parent interaction	• Shares purpose of learning activities • Shares learning objectives and what students will do to learn on a more regular basis • Holds some parent meetings (e.g., family night) to discuss learning goals and activities • Is beginning to create homework activities that all parents can do to support their child's learning	• Continuously and routinely shares purpose of learning activities with parents • Continuously provides learning objectives and what students will do to learn • Holds parent meetings to explain learning goals and activities • Infuses learning activities that can be done at home to support learning • Holds family events that support thinking-to-learn goals

Resource E. Observation Chart for the Sociocultural Frame

Grounds learning by (1) building strong relationships with students and families, (2) connecting curriculum with issues that are socially relevant for students, and (3) drawing from students' sociocultural strengths

Stage of professional development	Emerging	Developing	Enacting	Integrating
Builds relationships with students				
Builds relationships with parents				
Connects curriculum with students' lives to create a context-rich learning environment				
Connects curriculum with parents' lives to support learning in and out of school				
Engages students in paired and small-group work				

Observation Notes:

Date: _____

Resource F. Observation Chart for the Academic Language / Literacy Frame

Helps students develop strong language and literacy skills and ensures that parent communication is accessible				
Stage of professional development	Emerging	Developing	Enacting	Integrating
Pays attention to students' language and literacy development				
Makes learning understandable				
Models and provides consistent practice opportunities				
Assigns homework and assesses based on students' level of literacy				
Understands parents' academic language level				

Observation Notes:

Date: _____

Resource G. Observation Chart for the Academic Curricular Frame

Helps students develop strong academic/curricular skills and connects parents to the academic curriculum that their child is learning				
Stage of professional development	Emerging	Developing	Enacting	Integrating
Uses clear overarching unit and day's learning and language objectives				
Provides effective vocabulary instruction				
Provides challenging activities				
Provides modeling and practice opportunities				
Involves parents/families in their child's academic-curricular learning				

Observation Notes:

Date: _____

Resource H. Observation Chart for the Thinking-to-Learn Frame

Helps students develop strong cognitive thinking-to-learn skills and shares these with parents				
Stage of professional development	Emerging	Developing	Enacting	Integrating
Provides cognitive skill development to understand how we use language to express thinking				
Instructional conversation incorporates challenging, thought-provoking dialogues				
Uses visual organizers to support thinking-to-learn [skills]				
Involves parents/families in supporting their child's thinking-to-learn skills				
Provides modeling and practice opportunities				
Involves parents/families in their child's academic-curricular learning				

Observation Notes:

Date: _____

REFERENCES

Achieve. (2012). *About PARCC*. Retrieved from http://www.parcconline.org/about-parcc

Anderson, L. W., & Krathwohl, D. R. (Eds.). (2001). *A taxonomy for learning, teaching and assessing: A revision of Bloom's taxonomy of educational objectives.* New York, NY: Longman.

Balfanz, R., & Byrne, V. (2012). *Chronic absenteeism: Summarizing what we know from nationally available data.* Baltimore, MD: Johns Hopkins University, Center for Social Organization of Schools.

Bloom, B. S., & Krathwohl, D. R. (1956). *Taxonomy of educational objectives: The classification of educational goals, by a committee of college and university examiners. Handbook 1: Cognitive domain.* New York, NY: Longman.

Calderón, M. E., & Minaya-Rowe, L. (2011). *Preventing long-term ELs: Transforming schools to meet core standards.* Thousand Oaks, CA: Corwin.

Center for Research on Education, Diversity & Excellence. (2002). *A rubric for observing classroom enactments of CREDE's* Standards for Effective Pedagogy. Retrieved from http://gse.berkeley.edu/research/credearchive/standards/spac.shtml

Common Core State Standards Initiative. (2012). *Common standards.* Retrieved from http://www.corestandards.org/

Crane, S. (1895). *Red badge of courage.* New York, NY: D. Appleton.

Echevarria, J., Vogt, M. E., & Short, D. (2008). *Making content comprehensible for English learners: The SIOP model* (3rd ed.) Boston, MA: Allyn & Bacon.

Elmore, R. F. (2002). *Bridging the achievement gap between standards and achievement: The imperative for professional development in education.* Washington, DC: Albert Shanker Institute.

Halliday, M. A. K. (1973). *Explorations in the functions of language.* London: Edward Arnold.

Halliday, M. A. K. (1985). *Spoken and written language.* Oxford, England: Oxford University Press.

Halliday, M. A. K. (1993). Towards a language-based theory of learning. *Linguistics and Education, 5,* 93–116.

Kahneman, D. (2011). *Thinking fast and slow.* New York, NY: Farrar, Straus & Giroux.

Love, N., Stiles, K. E., Mudry, S., & DiRanna, K. (2008). *Unleashing the power of collaborative inquiry: The data coach's guide to improving learning for all students.* Thousand Oaks, CA: Corwin.

Pransky, K. (2008). *Beneath the surface: The hidden realities of teaching culturally and linguistically diverse young learners K–6.* Portsmouth, NH: Heinemann.

Research Center Report. (2011). Graduation in the United States: High school completion gains momentum. *Education Week: Diplomas Count, 30*(34), 26–27.

Smarter Balanced Assessment Consortium. (2012). *Smarter balanced assessments.* Retrieved from http://www.smarterbalanced.org/smarter-balanced-assessments/

Teemant, A. (2009). *English as a new language program rejoinder.* Retrieved from http://education.indiana.edu/tabid/13674/Default.aspx?fid=996

U.S. Department of Education. (2007). *State and local implementation of the No Child Left Behind Act: Volume III—Accountability under NCLB*. Retrieved from http://www2.ed.gov/rschstat/eval/disadv/nclb-accountability/nclb-accountability.pdf

Wayman, J. C., Midgley, S., & Stringfield, S. (2006). *Leadership for data-based decision-making: Collaborative educator teams*. Paper presented at the annual meeting of the American Education Research Association, San Francisco, CA. Retrieved from http://edadmin.edb.utexas.edu/datause/papers/Wayman-Midgley-Stringfield-AERA2006.pdf

Yoshikawa, H. (2011). *Immigrants raising citizens: Undocumented parents and their young children*. New York, NY: Russell Sage Foundation.

Zacarian, D. (2011). *Transforming schools for English learners: A comprehensive framework for school leaders*. Thousand Oaks, CA: Corwin.

Zacarian, D., & Haynes, J. (2012). *The essential guide for educating beginning English learners*. Thousand Oaks, CA: Corwin.

Index

CORWIN
A SAGE Company

The Corwin logo—a raven striding across an open book—represents the union of courage and learning. Corwin is committed to improving education for all learners by publishing books and other professional development resources for those serving the field of PreK–12 education. By providing practical, hands-on materials, Corwin continues to carry out the promise of its motto: **"Helping Educators Do Their Work Better."**